MW01139746

"I know pain, in:
times it almost c
for the kind of r<
Honestly, it's the. ....s meant for you. Ray Ortlund
tenderly explains how to find and embrace it in his excellent book *Good News at Rock Bottom*. I love Ray's style of writing—always accessible, believable, and gentle on the heart. The book you hold in your hands is extraordinary, and I envision that, by the last page, you will find the hope-filled release and relief you are yearning for."

Joni Eareckson Tada, Founder and CEO, Joni and Friends
International Disability Center

"Simeon had been waiting for the consolation of Israel, but what he found was Jesus (Luke 2:25), and that consolation from Christ soaks every page of this book. With understanding and tenderness, Ray Ortlund draws us back again and again to the all-sufficiency and matchless compassion of Christ. This is pastoral theology at its best—real, biblical, and deeply comforting."

Sam Allberry, Associate Pastor, Immanuel Nashville; author,
One with My Lord

"Whenever I feel I'm hitting rock bottom, Ray Ortlund is one of the first people I call. He doesn't cheerily wave away pain. He's seen what lurks in the darkness. Yet I always walk away hopeful and grateful and feeling alive again. That's because he knows the light that shines in the darkness. Reading this piercing book, you will experience the counsel of one who knows how bad it can get and who can help you see how good it can be."

Russell Moore, Editor in Chief, *Christianity Today*; author,
Losing Our Religion: An Altar Call for Evangelical America

"Ray Ortlund writes these words as a friend in the trenches with you, desperately needing God to be who he says he is in Isaiah 57:15. The night before I read this book, I was kept awake by loneliness, guilt, shame, and fear. The night after I read this, I was kept awake by the impossibility of processing how much God loves me. *Good News at Rock Bottom* was a love letter directly from God to me, through Ray. Trust me, read this! I'm already reading it again, with my wife and kids!"

Walker Hayes, singer; songwriter

"This gospel-saturated book has been so encouraging to me! I found myself nodding on every page as Ray Ortlund describes the pain of betrayal, the isolation of loneliness, the separation of sin, and the beautiful way God draws near to the brokenhearted. Ortlund underscores and illuminates this stunning truth: When we reach rock bottom, we find God is closer than we ever imagined and better than we ever dreamed. I highly recommend this book!"

Vaneetha Rendall Risner, author, *Desperate for Hope* and *Walking through Fire*

Good News at Rock Bottom

Crossway Books by Ray Ortlund

The Death of Porn: Men of Integrity Building a World of Nobility

The Death of Porn Study Guide: Men of Integrity Building a World of Nobility

Good News at Rock Bottom: Finding God When the Pain Goes Deep and Hope Seems Lost

The Gospel: How the Church Portrays the Beauty of Christ

Isaiah: God Saves Sinners

Marriage and the Mystery of the Gospel

Proverbs: Wisdom That Works

You're Not Crazy: Gospel Sanity for Weary Churches, with Sam Allberry

Good News
at Rock Bottom

Finding God When the Pain Goes
Deep and Hope Seems Lost

Ray Ortlund

WHEATON, ILLINOIS

Cover design: David Fassett

First printing 2025

Printed in the United States of America

Trade paperback ISBN: 978-1-4335-9886-9
ePub ISBN: 978-1-4335-9888-3
PDF ISBN: 978-1-4335-9887-6

Names: Ortlund, Raymond C., Jr., author.

Title: Good news at rock bottom : finding God when the pain goes deep and hope seems lost / Ray Ortlund.

Description: Wheaton, Illinois : Crossway, [2025] | Includes bibliographical references and index.

Identifiers: LCCN 2024023573 (print) | LCCN 2024023574 (ebook) | ISBN 9781433598869 (trade paperback) | ISBN 9781433598876 (pdf) | ISBN 9781433598883 (epub)

Subjects: LCSH: Bible. Gospels. | Christian life. | Depressed persons—Religious aspects—Christianity. | Anxiety—Religious aspects—Christianity.

Classification: LCC BS2555.55 .O87 2025 (print) | LCC BS2555.55 (ebook) | DDC 248.8/6—dc23/eng/20240911

LC record available at https://lccn.loc.gov/2024023573
LC ebook record available at https://lccn.loc.gov/2024023574

Crossway is a publishing ministry of Good News Publishers.

LB	34		33		32		31		30		29		28		27		26		25
15		14		13		12		11		10	9		8	7		6	5		4	3	2	1

To

Immanuel Church

and

St. Patrick's Anglican Church,
my dear friends in Christ

Contents

Preface

THANK YOU FOR PICKING UP this book. My plan here is to ask of you as little as I can and to give to you as much as I can. You have a busy life to live. But right now, while we are together, literally on the same page, let's make the most of it.

Here is what I promise you: I will try to explain the gospel of Jesus honestly and helpfully for your needs. I will not lie to you. And I will try to believe the gospel honestly and helpfully for my own needs.

Here is what I ask of you: Give Jesus a chance. Allow for the possibility that the good news about him is relevant to what you really, really care about—maybe more relevant than you have ever dared to believe.

So, my honest thoughts, with your courageous openness— let's see what happens.

This book began as a series of talks on Wednesday evenings at Immanuel Church, Nashville, in September 2023.

Immanuel is a church where people can heal. It's where I healed—and I was the pastor! So I wanted those talks to serve that gentle purpose. But still, I was surprised at the people's response. Something special was happening there in that room, and it was not me. It was more than all of us put together. It was the Lord himself, with the healing touch only he can bring.

Now I hope this book brings some of that healing to you too, by his grace, wherever you are, whatever you're facing.

And I wish I could give you a hug right now.

For thus says the One who is high and lifted up,
*   who inhabits eternity, whose name is Holy:*
"I dwell in the high and holy place,
*   and also with him who is of a contrite and lowly spirit,*
to revive the spirit of the lowly,
*   and to revive the heart of the contrite."*

ISAIAH 57:15

1

Way Up High, Way Down Low

YOU DON'T NEED TO GO looking for it. Sooner or later, it comes and finds you—something horrible, some experience unforeseeable and even unimaginable. It comes upon you. It lays hold of you. It changes you. And the reality you always understood to be your life—suddenly that life is gone for good. Now you're stuck with a different reality, and not one you chose. It was forced upon you. And however it happened, things are different for you now. And not in a better way.

I'm sorry to be dredging up bad memories for you. But if we sit quietly before the Lord for a while, I believe our hearts can crack open to something new—strong hope, deep healing,

> to revive the spirit of the lowly,
>   and to revive the heart of the contrite.

So, please don't close this book. I will be careful in everything I say. I have bad memories too.

What was it that came after you? Maybe it was betrayal. Someone won your heart. You trusted them, and you gave your heart away. But eventually, you found out they didn't really mean it. You did mean it—way down deep, too. But they didn't. Then you saw it, and it was a shock. To this day, the memory, the very thought, is still hard for you to bear. And they aren't coming back to apologize—ever. But your heart is still broken.

Or maybe it was a betrayal of your own. Maybe you were the one who crossed a line, knowing it was wrong. You were reaching for a thrill, to escape your boring life. You felt you deserved something exciting for a change. You wanted to find out if you still had what it takes. But that sin you picked up in your hands to play with, just for a while—now it *owns* you. You're trapped.

Or maybe it's nobody's fault. Maybe it's just the way your life has unfolded. It's like you've never found that place where you really belong, or that person you want to be with forever. Wherever you go, you feel like an outsider looking in. You don't hate your life. You have a lot to be thankful for. But you're lonely—every day.

Or maybe it's loss. For example, as you age. You don't just lose your job. You lose your youthful vigor, your very health.

You're not amazing anymore. You get tired just walking upstairs. And tomorrow will be *more* loss—maybe catastrophic loss. You look at yourself in the mirror and think, "Really? That's *me*?" And any time now, your life will be over.

We could go on and on. There are many ways to hit rock bottom. But everyone goes there. Which means you and I have a lot in common. Our broken hearts can bring us together. That's what I'm hoping for as you read this book.

We're in This Together

Neither of us wants to spiral down into self-pity. That doesn't help us, and it doesn't honor Christ. What you and I do want is enough hope to keep going with dignity. We want to face life as it is, upheld by Christ. Yes, we suffer anguish along the way. But we want to feel loved by him, as only survivors can.

We accept, we *deeply* accept, that there is no easy way through this world. But we want to walk *his* way, all the way. He himself is living proof that the cross leads to resurrection. His is the *only* way into the life that is truly life, even at rock bottom—especially at rock bottom. Our pain has become too real to settle for any theoretical "salvation." We're staking everything now on Jesus being real to the real us.

What if we follow Jesus together, you there and me here? We can find, to our surprise, that it's down at rock bottom where *he finds us*. In fact, the low place of loss and bewilderment and regrets and tears—*he's already down there*. It's where he dwells, where he awaits us and welcomes us.

It's not so bad down at rock bottom with Jesus there. And some really great people are down there too—the best people I've ever met. Welcome to the party! We weep at this party, but we laugh too. We laugh a lot. And we don't have to fake our joy. In fact, we wouldn't go back to our above-average lives for anything. We feel the way Martin Luther did.

> May a merciful God preserve me from a Christian Church in which everyone is a saint! I want to be and remain in the church and little flock of the fainthearted, the feeble and the ailing, who feel and recognize the wretchedness of their sins, who sigh and cry to God incessantly for comfort and help, who believe in the forgiveness of sins.[1]

There is a reason we talk about going to "a deeper place" with Christ. He meets us at our worst moments and our lowest defeats. He even takes us deeper than we thought we

---

1   Martin Luther, *Luther's Works*, vol. 22, *Sermons on the Gospel of St. John, Chapters 1–4* (St. Louis, MO: Concordia, 1957), 55, quoted in *1 Corinthians*, ed. Scott M. Manetsch, Reformation Commentary on Scripture (Downers Grove, IL: InterVarsity Press, 2017), 29.

needed to go. If we could have found an easier way, we would have settled for it! But since it's honest reality with Jesus we want, then the real us can be known *only* in the low place. Our false selves are exposed as frauds. It's painful. But our selfish dreams fading away to nothing—that's where Jesus surprises us with everything we really wanted all along. But he sure isn't the cheerleader of the triumphant winners. He is "a man of sorrows and acquainted with grief" (Isa. 53:3). He knows rock bottom firsthand. He *is* our good news at rock bottom.

The One Who Dwells with Us

What helps us most, when we need help urgently, is to discover *who Jesus is* for *people like us*. His wisdom is better than our escapism. What we want deep down is Jesus himself, with us, even us.

For example, Anselm, a theologian back in the eleventh century, had a conversation with himself one day. He dared to "change the subject" in his thoughts from his own turbulence to God. Anselm spoke bluntly to himself:

Come now, little man, flee for a moment from your preoccupations, escape for a while from your agitated thoughts. Put aside now your burdensome cares, and postpone your wearisome toils. Abandon yourself for a while to God, and rest a little in him. Enter into the resting place of your soul, shut out everything but God and what helps you to seek him. And after locking the door, seek him. Say now, O my whole heart, say now to God: "I seek your face. Your face, O Lord, I need."[2]

Whatever happened next, I'm guessing Anselm went on to have a good day! In our hyper-busy lives today, it can be even harder to get close to God. But rock bottom opens that door. We're finally desperate enough to shut the noise out and turn to him. We sure don't get to that profound place while sipping ice-cold lemonade on a sunny beach at Kiawah Island, do we? But when our hearts are crying out, "Your face, O Lord, I *need*," it's because we're in trouble. *So thank you, Lord, for trouble.*

C. S. Lewis said it well in one of his stories. Just this snippet of the dialogue makes the point:

"And what is this valley called?"

"We call it now simply Wisdom's Valley; but the oldest maps mark it as the Valley of Humiliation."[3]

2 Anselm, *St. Anselm's Proslogion*, trans. M. J. Charlesworth (Oxford: Clarendon, 1965), 110–11. I have changed the translation slightly.

3 C. S. Lewis, *The Pilgrim's Regress* (Grand Rapids, MI: Eerdmans, 1958), 125.

The Bible is an old map. It is honest, and hopeful. It's meant for real sufferers who wouldn't mind getting their lives back and having a future again. What then does the Bible have to say to people like us?

Where God Meets Us

> For thus says the One who is high and lifted up,
>   who inhabits eternity, whose name is Holy:
> "I dwell in the high and holy place,
>   and also with him who is of a contrite and lowly spirit,
> to revive the spirit of the lowly,
>   and to revive the heart of the contrite." (Isa. 57:15)

Let's do this: let's pick that verse up in our hands, turn it over and over like a priceless jewel, and see its facets of ancient wisdom from different angles. We can also think of it like a piece of hard candy. We pop it into our mouths, swirl it around with our tongues, and enjoy all the flavors.

The healing powers of this one verse can flow down into the deepest crevices of anguish within us. My plan, then, is to stare at Isaiah 57:15 for a while in each chapter of this book. We will keep gaining new insights along the way.

The great preacher Charles Spurgeon has been quoted as saying, "It is folly to think the Lord provides grace for every trouble but the one you are in today."[4] We are never helped by looking over at someone else and thinking, "I wish I had their life. Mine is such a letdown." The truth is, you *cannot* bear the burden of that wished-for life you'd gladly trade up to. Yes, it looks good. But it wasn't shaped to fit *you*. You'd end up hating it. And by God's grace, you *can* bear the burden of the actual life you're living. He is lifting you into your true dignity and destiny. And on your way there, you'll be encouraged by your fellow sufferers as they walk with you. I want this book to be one of those encouragements. If we savor Isaiah 57:15 *for the rest of our lives*, it will keep us going.

What, then, can we expect to happen, as the high and holy one dwells with us down at rock bottom?

First, let's notice the obvious: Isaiah 57:15 is about *God*. And for good reason. Our painful experiences raise *huge* questions about God. Like, "Where was he when I needed him most?" And the Bible doesn't always answer our questions. What it offers is a new way to hope and to worship—right where we are.[5]

4 I have been unable to confirm the source.
5 C. H. Spurgeon, "Job's Resignation," in *The Metropolitan Tabernacle Pulpit Sermons*, vol. 42 (London: Passmore and Alabaster, 1896), no. 2457: "O dear friend, when your grief presses you to the very dust, worship there!"

For example, the first thing we pray for in the Lord's Prayer is "Hallowed be your name" (Matt. 6:9). See that God-first priority? But "hallowed be your name" *isn't* the Lord implying, "I'll get around to *your* problems when I feel like it." He is saying to us, "You will be most helped in your pain today by looking to me first. Here I am, all that I am. I have real grace for the real you, as no one else does. But don't diminish the help I'm offering you by diminishing me." If God doesn't matter that much, we don't matter either. Nothing does.

But Isaiah 57:15 helps us see God, and ourselves, and everything in our lives that we hate—yes, *hate*—with new eyes. Let's take our verse line by line:

For thus says the One who is high and lifted up.

God is not silent. He has something big to say to us, something he wants us to be sure of. And Isaiah wrote it down, because he wants everyone, until the end of time, to know what God above has to say to people like us. Thank you, Isaiah! Truly, "there is something magnificent about these prophet-dreamers who are so sure of God."[6]

6 Ralph S. Cushman, *Practicing the Presence: A Quest for God* (Nashville: Abingdon, 1936), 108.

Isaiah is declaring this as a herald, a spokesman for the King. He calls us to give our full attention to a royal proclamation. As a point of comparison, when the brutal king of Assyria attacked Jerusalem, his emissary shouted, "Thus says the great king, the king of Assyria" (Isa. 36:4). Then he proceeded with his saber-rattling blah-blah-blah. But here, our kind King breaks through the angry noise of this world to speak to us. What's the message?

We can think of Isaiah 57:15 as the King's domestic policy. It isn't his mood in the moment—he isn't moody *at all*—but his settled posture toward us as we stumble our way, wounded and exhausted, into his kingdom. God has settled on an arrangement that does two beautiful things at once: it does justice to who God is, and it brings mercy to where we are. The one high and lifted up has mercies for us way down low. And he wants us to be *sure* of it.

In our world of lies and spin, this pronouncement from our faithful King stands out. Every day advertisers, governments, and even friends can lie to us. But what a relief it is to listen to the one far above all the heartbreaking fraudulence of this world! He alone is "Faithful and True" (Rev. 19:11). He doesn't *adhere* to that standard. He *is* the standard. The universe itself will have to implode before the Holy One will lie to us.

So, we're sitting on the edge of our seats, eager to listen.

But wait. Isaiah has more to say about our King. If he is "high and lifted up," what does that even mean? And how does his loftiness up there help us in our troubles down here?

"High and lifted up" doesn't mean God is spatially located above us—like we have to crane our necks to see him. God is spirit (John 4:24). He has no limits, no edges.[7] The Bible says, "Behold, heaven and the highest heaven cannot contain you" (1 Kings 8:27). In other words, the towering majesty of God transcends all our measurements—all inches, miles, light years. It was the pathetic pagan gods who were limited and localized. "Baal *of Peor*" (Num. 25:3), for example, was like a Mafia crime boss over in the Peor neighborhood.

Let's not slip into the same mentality today. If we cut Jesus down to size as our particular "take" on God, we are denying his greatness. He is no bobblehead "Jesus Junior"! To say he is "high and lifted up," the Bible is straining at the leash of language to describe him. Strong words like *majesty, splendor,*

7   John Calvin, *Institutes of the Christian Religion*, ed. John T. McNeill, trans. Ford Lewis Battles (Philadelphia: Westminster, 1960), 3.20.40: "He is not confined to any particular region but is diffused [expansive] through all things [*diffundi per omnia*]. . . . God is set beyond all place, so that when we would seek him we must rise above all perception of body and soul. . . . [He is] of infinite greatness or loftiness, of incomprehensible essence, of boundless might, and of everlasting immortality."

glory, and *greatness*[8] nudge our thoughts upward, toward his actual grandeur. He *exceeds* what we expect, even what we need. He is, and he deserves to be, our King. His "royal dignity"[9] is Isaiah's point.

We can be glad that God is "our Father *in heaven*" (Matt. 6:9). It means he is transcendent. Wherever life may take us, high or low, wonderful or horrible, God is already there, ready for us in all our need.

Let's improve our thoughts about God. The gentle J. I. Packer put it bluntly: "If you have been resigning yourself to the thought that God has left you high and dry, seek grace to be ashamed of yourself. Such unbelieving pessimism deeply dishonors our great God and Savior."[10] He is "of infinite power, wisdom, and goodness; the Maker, and Preserver of all things both visible and invisible."[11] He sure doesn't need any help from us, does he? *Only he* has "grace upon grace" (John 1:16) for our need upon need.

---

8 For example, "The LORD . . . is robed in majesty" (Ps. 93:1); "On the glorious splendor of your majesty / . . . I will meditate" (Ps. 145:5); Jesus is "the radiance of the glory of God" (Heb. 1:3); "Praise him according to his excellent greatness!" (Ps. 150:2).

9 John M. Frame, *The Doctrine of God* (Phillipsburg, NJ: P&R, 2002), 105.

10 J. I. Packer, *Knowing God* (Downers Grove, IL: InterVarsity Press, 1973), 79.

11 The Thirty-Nine Articles, 1, "Of Faith in the Holy Trinity," in *Creeds, Confessions, and Catechisms: A Reader's Edition*, ed. Chad Van DixHoorn (Wheaton, IL: Crossway, 2022), 115.

Years ago, J. B. Phillips, the brilliant Bible translator, wrote a book entitled *Your God Is Too Small*. In it he starts out with this insight: As we grow from childhood to adulthood, our concepts about reality grow bigger—our historical knowledge, our psychological awareness, our cultural sensitivities, and more. Our mental horizons get stretched in every direction. But if our thoughts of God aren't developed too, he starts looking smaller. He can even shrink to the vanishing point. And how can an adult worship a God who seems outclassed by everything else, especially everything terrifying? Phillips writes about each of us, "If, by a great effort of will, he does [keep believing in God], he will always be secretly afraid lest some new truth may expose the juvenility of his faith."[12]

We can't survive, much less flourish, with small thoughts of God. And God himself understands our need. It's why he gave us Isaiah 57:15. The one who is "high and lifted up" towers over everything that makes us feel small and defeated. But nothing about him can be offset by anything down in this world. He is not waiting for anybody's permission. He is not pushing against any door that won't open. As Martin Luther taught us to sing, our King reigns "above all earthly powers."[13]

12 J. B. Phillips, *Your God Is Too Small* (New York: Macmillan, 1953), v–vii.
13 "A Mighty Fortress Is Our God," *Worship and Service Hymnal* (Carol Stream, IL: Hope, 1957), 1.

We enjoy standing out under the stars on a clear night and looking up and marveling at the vast expanse of the universe. We feel tiny, but also calm. What if we gaze even higher and see God far above the universe itself? We start feeling even more tiny, and more calm. Whatever we're facing, seeing *God* more clearly helps us breathe a sigh of relief.

Now, line two:

. . . who inhabits eternity, whose name is Holy.

You and I experience reality in tiny increments, one moment after another, as time unfolds. But God, in his majestic eternality, is equally present to all points of time at once. For us, time means we have to wait—and we *hate* waiting. Amazon Prime built their success on our impatience! But God is never forced to wait. He isn't stuck inside time. He invented it and stands above it. Time *serves* him.

So there goes old Mr. Time out there, pottering around, doing God's will, slow as molasses—and God is okay with that. The upside is, God is always present in the moment with us. He is *always* right here right now. And as each new second breaks upon us, sometimes with a nasty surprise, God offers us eternal hope.

God "inhabits" eternity, Isaiah says. God *lives* there. God is *who* he is, *where* he is—which means he can attend to us, with no needs of his own. He is free at heart to be *all in* with us all the time.

What's more, ". . . whose name is Holy." His "name" is how he is rightly thought about and prayed to. His "name" makes him accessible. And surprisingly, his name "Holy" is a negative category. I don't mean it's a bad category. But "holy" means God *isn't* like us.

I am God and not a man,
the Holy One in your midst. (Hos. 11:9)

For example, the Bible describes God with many wonderful images—a lion, a rock, a shepherd, and so forth. But his name "Holy" means that all these metaphors, while they give us real insights into God, also fall short. Is he like a rock? Yes. How? He's steady and solid. But God is also tender. And no rock in this world is tender. And *everything* about God is "holy" like this—different, and better.

His holiness is not one more trait alongside others—his sovereignty, goodness, power, and so forth. *Everything* about God is holy—holy sovereignty, holy goodness, holy power, and all the rest of him. That's why his *name*, his very identity, is Holy—different, and better.

Let's always leave room for God to exceed our highest thoughts of him. Thinking about God is the noblest thing we ever do. But we will never wrap our brains around him completely. He will always keep surprising us.

Those are the first two lines of Isaiah 57:15. So far, we know that God stands over all creation, eternally unchanging, and better than our best thoughts of him.

Now, in lines three and four, the King himself speaks:

> I dwell in the high and holy place,
> and also with him who is of a contrite and lowly spirit.

Those two lines answer an urgent personal question: *When everything is on the line for us, where can we find God?* And the answer is, God can be found in two opposite places: way up high where we *can't* go, and way down low where we *can* go. "The high and holy place" is his royal palace in heaven above. It's a real place. The angels live there too. And the opposite place where God can be found is down with everyone who is "of a contrite and lowly spirit"—the devastated people at rock bottom. Here, then, are God's two addresses—up high, and down low.

But God does *not* make his dwelling place in between, in the social space I call "the mushy middle." We all understand that place. It's where people are doing pretty much okay. The kids are above average, the career is on track, and life is basically working. And "church" is a weekend option for upgrading an already pleasant life into an even more pleasant life, bumping up from maybe 6 to 7 on a scale of 1 to 10. That's the world I call "the mushy middle."

Many live there. Many more *want* to live there. It's where we finally get the prestige we want, the superiority, the control, the safe aloofness. It's where "the cool kids" hang out. And who wouldn't like to be invited to their parties?

Some churches cater to the mushy middle. Their "Jesus" is the chaplain to their status quo. He never judges, always approves, and squeezes uncomplainingly into the margin of their busy routines. He knows his place. In fact, he feels lucky to have their attention for one whole hour on a Sunday morning. But Isaiah sees a problem there. *The one who is high and lifted up, who inhabits eternity, whose name is Holy—the mushy middle is not his dwelling place.*[14]

Of course, God can get through to anyone anywhere. Some people in that world do love him. But life has not yet

14 Louis Berkhof, *Systematic Theology* (Grand Rapids, MI: Eerdmans, 1972), 134: "[God is] present in all His creatures, *but He is not present in every one of them in the same manner.*" Italics added.

forced them to discover *how real he is.* They might even look at someone who is "of a contrite and lowly spirit" and feel sorry for them. It's easy to go to church in the mushy middle, but it's hard to be awestruck by God there. The whole point of that world is to prop up a man-made heaven on earth. Here's the tragedy of that dreamy ideal:

> For though the LORD is high, he regards the lowly,
>   but the haughty he knows from afar. (Ps. 138:6)

> He who is mighty has done great things for me,
>   and holy is his name. . . .
> He has brought down the mighty from their thrones
>   and exalted those of humble estate;
> he has filled the hungry with good things,
>   and the rich he has sent away empty. (Luke 1:49, 52–53)

What about "contrite and lowly," then? Our very future hangs on those words. Here's what they mean. The word "contrite" means crushed, devastated, beaten down. And the word "lowly" means humiliated, demoted, diminished in worth.[15]

---

15 J. Alec Motyer, *Isaiah: An Introduction and Commentary* (Downers Grove, IL: InterVarsity Press, 1999), 358.

Those sufferings land us down at rock bottom—*right where the high and holy one dwells.*[16]

What is the high and holy God doing down with a bunch of losers? *What's going on at rock bottom?* He tells us in the last two lines of our verse:

> . . . to revive the spirit of the lowly,
> and to revive the heart of the contrite.

Whatever others might think of you, the risen Christ doesn't despise you. He isn't wondering when you'll finally "get it" and join the successful big shots of this world. The high and holy Christ is drawn tenderly to the injured, the despairing: "He offers life to those from whom the life has been all but crushed out; he offers life to those whose spirit has been ground down to nothing."[17]

What he *loves* to do is gently breathe hope back into us—not ambition to make it back into the mushy middle, but happiness to live near *him*, wherever *he* dwells. He revives us,

---

16 Herman Bavinck, *The Wonderful Works of God* (Glenside, PA: Westminster Seminary Press, 2019), 117: "*Precisely because* God is the High and Exalted One, and lives in eternity, He also dwells with those who are of a contrite and humble Spirit (Isaiah 57:15)." Italics added.

17 John N. Oswalt, *The Book of Isaiah: Chapters 40–66* (Grand Rapids, MI: Eerdmans, 1998), 488.

puts fresh heart into us, helping us to believe again that we have a life worth living, better than *anything* on a worldly scale of 1 to 10. He revives us by giving us himself more vividly than we've ever known before—*and* by giving us to one another.

I am adding "one another" into the picture now for a reason. "The lowly" and "the contrite" in these two lines are *plural* in the Hebrew text. God began by talking about an individual: "*him* who is of a contrite and lowly spirit." But now "the lowly" and "the contrite" are a group of people, *a community together down at rock bottom.* Drawn to him, we come together. We start experiencing real community— maybe for the first time.

What is he doing among us? He is wrapping his arms around us all, cherishing us has-beens and exiles as his own dear family. We're a mess, but we're *his* mess. That beautiful community is what we can experience every Sunday in a healthy church.

So we *love* rock bottom! *Jesus* is here. *We* are here. The most honest, gentle, and relaxed people anywhere are here. We wouldn't go back up to the mushy middle for all the money in the world!

We'll keep coming back to Isaiah 57:15. There's even more to enjoy.

Two Closing Thoughts

First, if your broken heart is starting to feel a little less isolated and more included, then maybe Charles Spurgeon can speak for you. Looking back at his conversion to Christ, he said:

> I felt that I could not be happy without fellowship with the people of God. I wanted to be wherever they were. And if anybody ridiculed them, I wished to be ridiculed with them. And if people had an ugly name for them, I wanted to be called by that ugly name. For I felt that, unless I suffered with Christ in his humiliation, I could not expect to reign with him in his glory.[18]

I hope your heart is saying that too. Mine sure is. I'm so done with fishing for approval from the wrong kind of people.

Second, if your heart is still crushed—deep injuries take time to heal—then here is a thought from Jesus himself. He said, "Let not your hearts be troubled. Believe in God; believe also in me" (John 14:1). God has told us, in Isaiah 57:15, that he dwells way up high and way down low. We can't *deserve*

---

18 C. H. Spurgeon, *Autobiography*, vol. 1, *The Early Years* (Edinburgh: Banner of Truth, 1985), 145.

someone like that. All he asks us to do is *believe* him. And when our faith opens up, his presence shows up.

This high and holy God, who dwells among the lowly, is *himself* lowly. Jesus said, "I am gentle and lowly in heart" (Matt. 11:29). No surprise, then, that he *loves* to dwell among the lowly. And he invites you to *believe* it: "Believe in God; believe also in me." Will you? He will lead you on from there.

So maybe a conversation has already begun between your wounded soul and the living Christ. It could go like this:[19]

SOUL. I'm so sad, so confused. I'm not sure what to think anymore.

CHRIST. Let not your heart be troubled. Believe in God; believe also in me.

SOUL. But you don't understand. I'm weak, unsteady. I will let you down.

CHRIST. Let not your heart be troubled. Believe in God; believe also in me.

SOUL. But what if you find in me some pretty crazy thoughts and feelings? On a bad day, I can be downright ridiculous.

---

19 I am borrowing this line of thought from John Bunyan, *Come and Welcome to Jesus Christ* (Edinburgh: Johnstone and Hunter, 1855), 147.

CHRIST. Let not your heart be troubled. Believe in God; believe also in me.

SOUL. Look, it's hard for me to admit this. But I happen to have some filthy habits you don't even want to know about.

CHRIST. Let not your heart be troubled. Believe in God; believe also in me.

SOUL. I get it! I get it! But if I agree, if I start believing in you, will you be patient with me while I stumble along the way?

CHRIST. Give me a chance. I will prove myself to you.

SOUL. Okay, then. Okay. I believe.

CHRIST. I'm all in. And I will never leave you nor forsake you.

Questions for Reflection and Discussion

1. It's hard to think about, I know. But what has been the worst rock-bottom experience in your life thus far? And what made it horrible for you?

2. Two surprising insights help us face our lives with new courage: (1) *who Jesus is*; (2) *where Jesus is*. Isaiah 57:15 explains both. Which aspects of this verse energize you the most? And why do you find them compelling?

23

3. People have reasons for wanting to live in "the mushy middle." Maybe there was a time when you wanted it too. If so, what was it about that world that you most desired for yourself? And what, by now, have you lost?

4. "Contrite and lowly" tends not to appear on our lists of life goals or career ambitions! But as you're thinking it through, how are those two categories becoming more hopeful and even desirable?

5. The word "revive" might, initially, suggest old-fashioned tent meetings and odd religious fervor. But Isaiah had better things in mind. How would you describe the picture he is painting with this word "revive"?

6. Looking at Isaiah 57:15 as a whole, and with your rock-bottom suffering in mind—if God offered you just one part of this life-giving scenario Isaiah describes, which aspect would you ask him for? And why *that* gift?

7. Maybe at this point you'd like to write out a prayer. You can lift your desire to God right now. Use your own words. He understands. In fact, he fixes our prayers on their way up!

For thus says the One who is high and lifted up,
    who inhabits eternity, whose name is Holy:
"I dwell in the high and holy place,
    and also with him who is of a contrite and lowly spirit,
to revive the spirit of the lowly,
    and to revive the heart of the contrite."

ISAIAH 57:15

2

Betrayed

WHEN OUR LIVES FALL APART, and we really need help, and we wonder if we can even keep going, *where can we find God?*

As we've seen, the Bible says that God dwells in two opposite places at once—way up high in his holy place above, where we can't go, and way down low among the lowly and contrite, where we can go. But it can be hard to find God in the mushy middle.

That world of privilege and advantage, where money has the power to keep trouble out and pleasure in, where we can be "successful" without God—that false heaven is a comfortable trap. It trivializes Jesus as a lifestyle enhancement. He is not high and lifted up, not eternal and holy. He just doesn't count for *that* much.

Isaiah 57:15 changes how we perceive *him*, which also changes where *we* want to live. Wherever he is—that's where we'll find all that we truly need. Our Lord must be easy to find way up there in his heavenly glory. The angels are awestruck by him 24/7! Our Lord is also easy to find way down low at our rock bottom. So many saints can attest to that! But that middle space of worldly desires, with traffic jams of U-Hauls crowding in to move there every day—you and I see it differently now, don't we?

Now that it's *God* we want, rock bottom can start looking like the garden of Eden.

King David understood. He tells of when his very life was hanging by a thread:

I cried aloud to the LORD,
    and he answered me from his holy hill. (Ps. 3:4)

Let's not miss the surprising geography—both literal and metaphorical—in that verse.

Psalm 3:4 pictures God atop holy Mount Zion, twenty-five hundred feet above sea level. As he prays this psalm David is in the Jordanian Rift, nearly twenty-five hundred feet below sea level—literally the lowest point on earth.

. . . The language is intended to draw attention both to the depths of David's plight and to the transcendent God who rules over all.[1]

Apparently, our Savior loves these extremes—up high, down low. It must mean that he is not too glorious to bother with us down here; he is too glorious *not* to care about us.

Sadly, not every place that passes as "Christian" will help us. Some might break our hearts even more deeply. But putting all our hope in the real Jesus, we take our stand here. "If your religion doesn't help you, it is no religion for you; you had better be without it."[2] Therefore, we gladly *descend* to God's dwelling place, where he brings real help for real sufferers.

Isaiah 57:15 is good news, isn't it? When we've lost so much that we fear we're stuck now with a Plan B existence—*that scenario is where God dwells*. As we stumble into his healing presence, he greets us with a gentle question: "Would you like a hug?" Remember that father whose longing heart waited for his knucklehead prodigal son to come back home? "His father saw him and felt compassion, and ran *and embraced*

1 Bruce K. Waltke and Fred G. Zaspel, *How to Read and Understand the Psalms* (Wheaton, IL: Crossway, 2023), 55.

2 Mark Rutherford, *The Revolution in Tanner's Lane* (New York: Cape and Smith, 1929), 266.

him and kissed him" (Luke 15:20). Would *you* like that hug from your Father?

Maybe you're still uneasy. Maybe you suspect that what God really wants is to chew you out: "If you'd been paying attention, you wouldn't be down here!" But the Bible says the opposite. What God wants is to "revive" the spirit of the crushed and the devastated. What he wants is to *breathe fresh life* into you. And Isaiah 57:15 is not exaggerating. Its hopeful message is not even exceptional. This verse is *vintage Bible truth.*

James Muilenburg, in his 1956 commentary on Isaiah, writes, "The whole New Testament provides a running commentary on these words."[3] And John Oswalt, in his 1998 commentary, calls Isaiah 57:15 "one of the finest one-sentence summations of biblical theology in the Bible."[4]

Earlier in the Old Testament, Psalm 34 says,

The LORD is near to the brokenhearted
and saves the crushed in spirit. (Ps. 34:18)

3   James Muilenburg, "The Book of Isaiah," in *The Interpreter's Bible*, ed. George A. Buttrick, vol. 5, *Ecclesiastes, Song of Songs, Isaiah, Jeremiah* (New York: Abingdon, 1956), 672.

4   John N. Oswalt, *The Book of Isaiah: Chapters 40–66* (Grand Rapids, MI: Eerdmans, 1998), 487.

And "the crushed in spirit" there translates the same wording as "contrite" does in Isaiah 57:15. God is not aloof from devastated people, but he is very near: "The Lord Jesus knows what it is to be crushed in spirit."[5]

But Psalm 34 also says, "The face of the LORD is against those who do evil" (v. 16). They "do evil" by choosing ease, control, and big-deal-ness rather than the Father's embrace. The mushy middle is where they *want* to dwell, precisely because God *doesn't* dwell there. That desire is evil. And it breeds more evils, as we see every day in this world.

C. S. Lewis explains the staggering choice confronting every one of us:

> We are warned that it may happen to any one of us to appear at last before the face of God and hear only the appalling words, "I never knew you. Depart from me." . . . We can be left utterly and absolutely outside—repelled, exiled, estranged, finally and unspeakably ignored. On the other hand, we can be called in, welcomed, received, acknowledged.[6]

---

5 Dane Ortlund, *In the Lord I Take Refuge: 150 Daily Devotions through the Psalms* (Wheaton, IL: Crossway, 2021), 94.

6 C. S. Lewis, *The Weight of Glory and Other Addresses* (Grand Rapids, MI: Eerdmans, 1974), 12.

Here is what Jesus said about the lowly and contrite who collapse in the Father's arms: "Blessed are the poor in spirit, for theirs is the kingdom of heaven" (Matt. 5:3). That word "blessed" is not a pious cliché. That strong word is a joyous high five. Jesus is *congratulating* the poor in spirit. He looks at them with beaming approval and says, "Way to go!" Who are those lucky guys? Who are those who end up not on the bench but out on the field with the team, celebrating their come-from-behind championship victory, and then in the locker room are shaking up bottles of champagne and spraying each other for the sheer joy of it all, and then are going out together to the postgame party and dancing the night away? Who gets in on *that* joy? Not the swaggering big shots of this world. Jesus ignores them. But the true celebrants are the poor in spirit, who have nothing to offer him but their defeat. He congratulates *them* as the winners. He welcomes *them* into his kingdom. They are where the high and holy one dwells.

Having him near is our only "success"—if that's even the right word for it. To everyone with enough regrets to know that his grace is their last hope, Jesus opens up *the treasures of himself* forever. And the smug insiders up in their self-exalting middle space? All they have is *themselves*, and *forever*.

Here's one more New Testament verse, near the very end of the Bible: "Let *the one who is thirsty* come; let *the one who desires* take the water of life without price" (Rev. 22:17). All you need is need—like burning thirst, like unsatisfied desire. Where Christ dwells, your lack is your wealth. *Don't wish it away. Bring it to him. Keep on bringing it to him.* He invites *you* to come, and he invites *you* to take—without price. He has already paid the price at his cross. As Spurgeon said, "When Jesus is the host, no guest goes empty from the table."[7]

What cracks our hearts open more deeply to his love is our loss of everything except his love. There, in our devastation, he welcomes us with happiness that's real and purpose that's satisfying. It's the real life he wanted for us from the start.

The legendary Barbra Streisand said that, after she has recorded an album, she's so tired of the songs that "I never listen to my records for maybe 10 years. . . . Really, I just get sick of it." She added, "That's why I gave up concerts. . . . It's boring to sing your own songs."[8] We are all pretty boring, aren't we? But Jesus *revives* our spirits. That's why Isaiah 57:15 is in poetic form. Did you notice that? The verse isn't prose. It's poetry. How could such a hope *not* be expressed in poetry? Something so improbable, so glorious—that the

7 Charles Haddon Spurgeon, *Morning and Evening* (1874; repr., Grand Rapids, MI: Zondervan, 1955), March 19, evening.

8 "Streisand 'Bored by Her Own Songs,'" *BBC News*, September 24, 2003, http://news.bbc.co.uk/2/hi/entertainment/3134596.stm.

all-holy God above comes all the way down to dwell with us at our lowest, giving his best to this world's least—it takes poetry to say that!

Isn't Isaiah 57:15 an amazing verse!

Now, let's shine the light of this hope into a dark place inside every one of us: the pain of betrayal. One of the common ways we land down at rock bottom is by our trust being betrayed and our hearts deeply broken. How does God dwell among us, with his heart-reviving help, *then*?

What Is Betrayal?

Betrayal is *not* the same thing as disappointment. The distinction is important. I don't want to accuse someone of betrayal if all they've done is disappoint me. Disappointment might be my own fault. Maybe my own made-up expectations were dashed. That picture I painted in my mind didn't come true. It's not their fault.

Betrayal is different. Betrayal is not dashed expectations but broken promises—promises someone else declared to you or to me, clearly and freely. And that *is* serious, and seriously injurious.

Betrayal is when a person or a group or an institution makes promises to you, and you believe their promises. You open up and get close to those people, you give them your heart, so that something deep within you is at stake in your relationship with them. But then they break their word. They violate your trust. And they might even blame it on you, in order to justify themselves. You come to realize that what really matters to them is their narrative of successful grandiosity. And when they have to choose between your rights and their narrative, you just don't matter anymore. Their commitments to you go "poof," nothing real is there, and you are thrust out. That's betrayal.

Some obvious examples: wedding vows are broken by infidelity or abandonment; confidential information about you is leaked and you are publicly humiliated; a friendship you thought was heartfelt turns out to be a cost-benefit calculation, and you discover that you are expendable; a friend fails to stick up for you when you come under attack, and your friend chooses instead to keep a low profile and wait it out until the trouble blows over. Betrayal takes many forms. But it always involves violated trust. The pain goes deep.

For me, this isn't theoretical. It's how I hit rock bottom. My experience of betrayal was bewildering. Growing up in a happy home and a healthy church, marrying my amazing wife, having our precious children, and enjoying the Christian ministry—I had never experienced the knife thrust of betrayal down at a primal level of my being. The injury was profound.

For example, I had always been a sound sleeper. But now I found myself waking up at night, maybe two or three times a week, hallucinating. Startled awake, I would see intruders coming into our bedroom, like through the ceiling or through a crack in the wall that isn't even there. And for fifteen or twenty seconds, these intruders, coming in like assassins, seemed utterly real. To this day, I can't relax and go upstairs to bed at night until I've checked all the locks on the doors. I lock our bedroom door too. And I still feel anxiety when I lie down to go to sleep. It's crazy, I know. Rationally, the security of our home is obvious. But emotionally, I've never found that "off" button to push and make it go away. Jani and I live in a safe neighborhood. But that reality is overruled by something deeper inside me.

If that's you too, then I'm seeing an upside for us here. We're in this mess *together*. Thank you for reading this book. Thank you for trusting me and giving me a chance. One of the positive outcomes of that anguish in my life is a gift God gave me down at rock bottom. To me, it's a precious gift. And I could not have received this gift anywhere else. But down there, God put inside me an intense desire to care for people, reassure people, protect people. He pressed into my heart a deep determination that *no one* within my range of influence is ever going to be mistreated. No way! By God's grace, my presence is going to be a safe place where injured people can relax and heal, for God's glory.

Betrayal reminds us of Judas Iscariot, of course. The verb in the New Testament that describes what Judas did to Jesus— a terrible word Judas himself uses, translated "betray" (NASB) or "deliver" (ESV) in Matthew 26:15—means hand someone over, give someone up, abandon them. In other words, the betrayer takes control.[9] That's more than disappointing. It's terrifying.

Why Does Betrayal Shatter Us So Deeply?

Betrayal crushes us, because *real* relationships are built on trust. Real friendship is grounded in the solid bedrock of steady faithfulness we can count on through thick and thin. When we trust someone, we take a risk. We hand over to them something of ourselves deep within. We become vulnerable. If our trust is then violated, it isn't just our plans that get changed. Our hearts get broken. It couldn't be more personal—and sharply felt.

The Bible helps us understand *why* so much is at stake in these bonds we form together. We are not trivial beings, not

9   *The Cambridge Greek Lexicon*, ed. James Diggle, 2 vols. (Cambridge: Cambridge University Press, 2021), 2:1065: "hand over (what is in one's charge or possession) to another."

the way God created us. And the glory of it all shines most brightly in our relationships—or it should, anyway. Scripture shows us the way-down-deep glory, *the divine glory*, in faithful human relationships. We see it again and again in one of the Bible's central themes: *covenant*.

For example, the preface to the whole Bible is Genesis 1–11. There God says to Noah, "I will establish my covenant with you" (Gen. 6:18). What was God doing by saying that? He was *committing himself*. He didn't have to. Nobody even asked him to. But God got involved—willingly, sincerely. He obligated himself, so that he couldn't back out, no matter what it would cost him.[10] Why would God stick his neck out like that? Because he cares. He really does care about this train-wreck world. And he's committed to taking us all the way, to where our happiness will never end.

Rock-solid covenantal faithfulness—God sums up the beauty of it when he says to us, as he does repeatedly, "I will be your God, and you will be my people" (see Gen. 17:7; Ex. 6:7; etc.). In other words, "Here is my solemn promise to you, always and forever. I will be *God* to you—for all that God is

10 Bruce K. Waltke, *An Old Testament Theology: An Exegetical, Canonical, and Thematic Approach* (Grand Rapids, MI: Zondervan, 2007), 287: "*Covenant* means 'a solemn commitment of oneself to undertake an obligation.'"

worth. And you will be *my people*—my own dear ones. We will *always* be together, whatever it costs me." And here is my point. Doing life together in that covenantal way is the big, wraparound category for everything else in the whole Bible (Gal. 3:15–29). It is *the* key insight into the God-defined reality we are living in.

Here's why I think that's amazing. *Covenant* means that we've parachuted into a universe where Ultimate Reality is not politics, not even physics, but relationships—personal, lasting, beautiful relationships of promises made and promises kept. It's *who God is*, and who God made *us* to be. Other gods aren't covenantal. "The idea of a covenant between a deity and a people is unknown to us from other religions and cultures."[11] Covenant living is uniquely Christian. And if a covenant-keeping God created us to be covenant-keeping people together, then violating trust is not only the betrayal of a friend. It is a stab in God's back.

Let's *all* admit how we've let others down. But part of God's covenant with us is to help us even there. He promises to create in us new hearts that *will* do the right thing, no matter what (Jer. 31:31–34).

11 Moishe Weinfeld, "bᵉrith," *Journal of the American Oriental Society* 90 (1970): 278, quoted in Waltke, *An Old Testament Theology*, 148.

The bottom line is this. Covenantal relationships of commitment and trust are not a human invention we can modify for our convenience. The beauty of costly faithfulness is a divine gift worthy of our reverence. Covenantal living is essential to human flourishing. We live together in community by making promises and keeping promises. God dignifies *all* our relationships with one another with covenantal dynamics.

Here's how practical it gets. When I walk into a room, in that moment I literally owe everyone there my best. And they owe me their best. We aren't always good at it. But let's be clear in our resolve to be faithful to one another, by God's grace. *The essence of our beauty together is a "you can count on me" vulnerability.*

When your trust was violated, you weren't crazy to feel how much was really on the line. Something truly worthy was being trashed. Keeping our word with one another glorifies God and honors people. But betrayal is living hell.

Somewhere I heard Jordan Peterson point out that, in Dante's *Inferno*, the deepest level of hell is reserved for treacherous people guilty of betrayal. And their hell is not a lake of fire but of ice. One Dante scholar explains: "This is Dante's symbolic equivalent of the final guilt. The treacheries of these souls were denials of love and of all human warmth. Only the remorseless dead center of the ice will serve to express their natures."[12] No wonder you found betrayal utterly chilling. What came after you was seriously evil.

There is only one thing more costly than giving our hearts away. And that is *not* giving our hearts away at all. In his classic work *The Four Loves*, C. S. Lewis helps us see the alternatives always before us:

> To love at all is to be vulnerable. Love anything, and your heart will certainly be wrung and possibly be broken. If you want to make sure of keeping it intact, you must give your heart to no one, not even to an animal. Wrap it carefully round with hobbies and little luxuries; avoid all entanglements; lock it up safe in the casket or coffin of your selfishness. But in that casket—safe, dark, motionless, airless—it will change. It will not be broken; it will become unbreakable, impenetrable, irredeemable. The alternative to tragedy, or at least to the risk of tragedy, is damnation. The only place outside Heaven where you can be perfectly safe from all the dangers and perturbations of love is Hell.[13]

12 Dante Alighieri, *The Divine Comedy: Inferno*, trans. John Ciardi (New York: Modern Library, 1996), 270.

13 C. S. Lewis, *The Four Loves* (New York: Harcourt, Brace, Jovanovich, 1960), 169.

Thank you for giving your heart away. Even though your trust was broken, still, you stepped into covenant. You did the Christlike thing. Way to go! The Lord will honor you for staying true to him when it was costly.

> This is the message that you have heard from the beginning, that we should love one another. We should not be like Cain, who was of the evil one and murdered his brother. And why did he murder him? Because his own deeds were evil and his brother's righteous. (1 John 3:11–12)

Maybe you weren't perfect in that covenant relationship. But you were Christian. In fact, *that was your crime.* It was your integrity that made you someone's sacrificial lamb.

How Does Jesus Meet Us Down at the Rock Bottom of Betrayal?

Here I have good news for you, but I also have bad news for you.

Let's start with the good news. *Jesus himself suffered betrayal, he felt the horror of it, and he's going to do something about it.*

That's *why* the high and holy one dwells down at rock bottom. There is no way he is going to let you go through that suffering alone. He feels it deeply.

God is also angry about what happened to you. He is angry at *all* injustice, *every* betrayal, *any time* wrongs are done to another. He knows exactly how you were wronged, and he stands against injustice. But God gets good and angry. His response to evil is to do the greatest good thing the world has ever seen. He sends his own Son as a man of sorrows who enters and knows our suffering.[14]

B. B. Warfield, the Princeton theologian of a century ago, in his brilliant essay "The Emotional Life of Our Lord," writes, "Jesus burned with anger against the wrongs he met with in his journey through human life as truly as he melted with pity at the sight of the world's misery: and it was out of these two emotions that his actual mercy proceeded."[15]

Our Lord's love for us includes his anger at the wrongs done to us. It's why the apostle Paul wrote about a villainous man who betrayed him, "The Lord will repay him according to his deeds" (2 Tim. 4:14). Paul didn't have to indulge in personal payback. The wrath of God is all the wrath this world needs!

---

14 David Powlison, *Good and Angry: Redeeming Anger, Irritation, Complaining, and Bitterness* (Greensboro, NC: New Growth, 2016), 174. Italics his.

15 B. B. Warfield, *The Emotional Life of Our Lord* (Wheaton, IL: Crossway, 2022), 76.

Should we too feel anger at betrayal? Yes. Anger is a judging emotion. And we are not wrong to feel that evil should be judged. But, sadly, the evil that betrays—that evil is lurking inside us too. *God's* wrath is perfect. *Our* wrath is flawed. Let's trust him to do the right thing in the right way, and let's be cautious about ourselves. Let's not turn a blind eye, but let's not lash out either. Let's trust our covenantal God to settle every score in his own time and in his own way. He's good at dealing out whatever punishments he knows are best, now and forever.[16]

The wrath of God is *good news* for everyone who cares about justice in this world. He meets us at rock bottom with his solemn promise that *no one is getting away with anything*—not on his watch! "Shall not the Judge of all the earth do what is just?" (Gen. 18:25). That's the good news.

Now here's the bad news. You might not want to hear it. I don't. But here we go. *At some point, you and I have to start forgiving our betrayers.* You don't have to trust them or like them or hang out with them. But you do have to forgive them—or start the journey into forgiving them. So do I.

Isn't that how our Lord taught us to pray?

16 Miroslav Volf, *Exclusion and Embrace: A Theological Exploration of Identity, Otherness, and Reconciliation* (Nashville: Abingdon, 2019), 298: "The certainty of God's just judgment at the end of history is the presupposition for the renunciation of violence in the middle of it."

Forgive us our debts,

as we also have forgiven our debtors. (Matt. 6:12)

There it is, as clear as day. He said it again: "If you forgive others their trespasses, your heavenly Father will also forgive you" (Matt. 6:14). We don't *earn* his forgiveness of us by forgiving others. We *prove* his forgiveness of us by forgiving others. We enter into Christ by being forgiven, and we display Christ by forgiving others.

It might take a long time. It might feel like you have to forgive over and over again, because the injury flares up over and over again. Jesus spoke of forgiving not seven times but "seventy-seven times" (Matt. 18:22). We might have to remind ourselves repeatedly that God's anger is better than our anger. And after seventy-seven times, we might *start* to feel it and relax and forgive. But our Lord—not our betrayer finally owning up, but our Lord himself right now, with his grace and his wrath—is why we can open up to forgiving our betrayer.

What is forgiveness? It is deciding we will *not* make the traitors pay for what they did. Look how our Lord puts it: "as we forgive our *debtors*" means that they *owe* us. What they took from us they should restore to us. But forgiveness means we absorb the impact of their wrong. We accept the losses we suffered because of their evil. We trust God to turn the wreckage into beauty we can scarcely imagine. His covenant faithfulness will overrule their betrayal, bending it around in the opposite direction. He will take us further into what we really want than we ever could have achieved by a comfortably undisturbed mushy-middle existence.

Forgiveness means that, if they *are* going to suffer for their betrayal, it won't be us dishing it out. It will be the high and holy one, who is well able to bring them down to rock bottom with us, where they might even come clean. Maybe right now they're too hard-hearted, too proud. But if they *can* be saved, Jesus is the one to do it. And if they can't—well, you and I are hardly qualified to damn anybody.

Our privilege, as covenantal people in this generation— *what we literally owe everyone*—is to keep trusting the Lord and keep doing the right thing, even when it's hard, especially when it's hard. And the right thing, so often, is to be merciful. Inevitably, our Lord calls us to be more merciful than we ever dreamed we'd have to be. But if, in the moment of decision, I turn away from the Lord, if I put my foot down and *refuse* to forgive, then I am *adding* to the evil in the world. I am giving the one who betrayed me more power over me. Mercy is serious, isn't it? But it's also freeing.

Here's a true story of Christlike forgiveness. Corrie ten Boom was a devout Christian in Holland during World

War II. Her family secretly sheltered Jews from the Nazis. But the family was betrayed and sent to concentration camps. Her sister Betsie died in that horrible place, but Corrie survived.

Soon after the war, Corrie was speaking at a Christian meeting in Germany. Her topic was forgiveness. "When we confess our sins," she said, "God casts them into the deepest ocean, gone forever. God then places a sign out there that says, 'No Fishing Allowed.' "[17]

As the meeting ended and people were quietly filing out, Corrie saw a man approaching her. Suddenly she realized—he had been one of the most sadistic guards in that prison. But now here he was again, this time his hand outstretched, asking her, "Will you forgive me?" Corrie froze. "I stood there—I whose sins had again and again to be forgiven—and could not forgive. Betsie had died in that place—could he erase her slow terrible death simply for the asking?"

The sufferings that man had inflicted were real. And now he was asking, "Will you forgive me?"

She continues:

"Jesus, help me!" I prayed silently. "I can lift my hand. I can do that much. You supply the feeling." And so woodenly,

---

17 Corrie ten Boom, *Tramp for the Lord* (Fort Washington, PA: CLC, 1974), 55–57.

47

mechanically, I thrust my hand into the one stretched out to me. And as I did, an incredible thing took place. The current started in my shoulder, raced down my arm, sprang into our joined hands. And then this healing warmth seemed to flood my whole being, bringing tears to my eyes. "I forgive you, brother," I cried. "With all my heart." For a long moment we grasped each other's hands, the former guard and the former prisoner. I had never known God's love so intensely as I did then.

Can we think of anything more healing in this brutal world than real forgiveness? We have no future without it. And rock bottom is where a better world *is* beginning to appear, a new world where God's power to forgive redefines our future.

In his book *People of the Lie*, M. Scott Peck helps us understand the power of God's mercy through us:

The healing of evil . . . can be accomplished only by the love of individuals. A willing sacrifice is required. The individual healer must allow his or her own soul to become the battleground. He or she must sacrificially *absorb* the evil. . . . There is a mysterious alchemy whereby the victim becomes the victor. As C. S. Lewis wrote, "When a willing victim who had committed no treachery was killed in a traitor's stead, the Table would crack and Death itself would start working backwards." I do not know how this occurs. But I know that it does. I know that good people can deliberately allow themselves to be pierced by the evil of others—to be broken thereby yet somehow not broken—to even be killed in some sense and yet still survive and not succumb. *Whenever this happens, there is a slight shift in the balance of power in the world.*[18]

You are never more like Jesus, never more powerful, than when you forgive the real evil that ruined your life. That merciful you is the most alive you, the most beautiful you, the most consequential you that could exist in this generation. And that tear-stained, glorious you, down there at rock bottom, is shifting the balance of power in this world away from evil and toward the high and holy one, by his grace, for his glory.

You might be doing better than you think.

Maybe way better.

18 M. Scott Peck, *People of the Lie: The Hope for Healing Human Evil* (New York: Simon and Schuster, 1983), 269. Italics added.

Questions for Reflection and Discussion

1. As you continue to reflect on Isaiah 57:15, what is one new thought about God that stands out to you with special clarity? And how does that new insight help you in a practical way?

2. What was the occasion, or the moment, or the relationship when your trust was the most betrayed? I am sorry to ask. But let's remember: Jesus is the most present right where your heart is the most broken.

3. The concept of *covenant* is the heart of the Bible. God made promises to us, and God keeps his promises, even at cost to himself. For example, he said, "I will be your God, and you will be my people." Put into your own words what that promise means to you, how that promise lifts your heart.

4. In the ongoing struggle to forgive your betrayer, Jesus supports you. It isn't easy to forgive over and over again, as painful memories come flooding back. But how can you trust your Savior to help you in those hard moments?

5. Write a list of the people with whom you are in covenant—your spouse, family members, friends at church,

close neighbors, teammates, military comrades, business associates, others. With each name, write down one particular covenantal obligation you owe. In addition, write the specific way you intend, by God's grace, to stay faithful to each person.

6. Finally, standing back and looking at chapter 2 as a whole—the heartbreak of human betrayal and the assurance of God's covenant faithfulness to you—how can that realism and that hope help you take a new step into your future, by God's grace?

7. At this point in your journey, what prayer do you want to lift to God? You can do so right now, in your own words, from your heart to his.

For thus says the One who is high and lifted up,
   who inhabits eternity, whose name is Holy:
"I dwell in the high and holy place,
   and also with him who is of a contrite and lowly spirit,
to revive the spirit of the lowly,
   and to revive the heart of the contrite."

ISAIAH 57:15

3

Trapped

ONE OF SATAN'S OLDEST TRICKS is this: *he shows the bait, but he hides the hook.*[1] We understand that from painful experience, don't we? We know by now that sin is no thrill ride. It's more like a bad time-share deal—easy to get in, hard to get out, and not even much fun while we're there. Still worse, mere willpower alone can't get our freedom back.

Jesus was realistic about our sins—how deeply that hook digs into us. He said, "Everyone who practices sin is *a slave* to sin" (John 8:34). Peter too was blunt: "Whatever overcomes a person, to that he is enslaved" (2 Pet. 2:19). Paul warned us that we can "fall into the devil's trap"

[1] Thomas Brooks, *Precious Remedies against Satan's Devices* (Edinburgh: Banner of Truth, 2011), 29.

(1 Tim. 3:7, NLT). But Jesus also said, "If the Son sets you free, you will be free indeed" (John 8:36). We *don't* have to stay stuck where we are. C. S. Lewis helps us to become decisive: "It's not a question of God 'sending' us to Hell. In each of us there is something growing up which will of itself *be Hell* unless it is nipped in the bud. The matter is serious. Let us put ourselves in His hands at once—this very day, this hour."[2]

Here is our hope. *Jesus is moving down among the lowly and contrite with liberating power.* Let's not deny how low we've fallen. Is rock bottom what we want? No. But is it also his address? Yes. Right here he is offering us a freedom we never could experience back up in our smug mushy-middle, blah-whatever, barely existing existence.

More Insight from Isaiah 57:15

Before we jump in, here's another detail in Isaiah 57:15 just itching to bless us. It's the first word: "*For* thus says the One who is high and lifted up." How does that little word make a big difference? It takes some explaining.

As we've seen, the high and holy one has two dwelling places: way up high, and way down low. Our verse is *not*

2 C. S. Lewis, *God in the Dock: Essays on Theology and Ethics*, ed. Walter Hooper (Grand Rapids, MI: Eerdmans, 1970), 155. Italics his.

explaining why God chooses those two opposite places. But our verse *is* explaining why God is going public about it. He wants us to *know* where we can find him.

This opening word "for" gets us looking back at the context. And verse 14 emphasizes how strongly God feels about getting close to us. He *really* wants us to know that he isn't avoiding us but is near to us. In fact, God is throwing the doors wide open.

And it shall be said,
   "Build up, build up, prepare the way,
   remove every obstruction from my people's way."
      (Isa. 57:14)

"And it shall be said." Okay, but "said" by whom? To whom? "There is an air of mystery and solemnity about this."[3] But even the ambiguity makes a point. *One way or another*, God is going to make sure that his open invitation gets out to us, wherever we are: "And it *shall* be said."

The rest of verse 14 is a declaration from our King. It's Jesus talking, echoed by the apostles and prophets and all his faithful voices through the centuries. The message is this:

3 J. Alec Motyer, *The Prophecy of Isaiah: An Introduction and Commentary* (Downers Grove, IL: InterVarsity Press, 1993), 475.

our Lord's heart is for broken people, the new beginning he wants for us.

Here is his plan:

> Build up, build up, prepare the way,
>> remove every obstruction from my people's way.

It's the picture of a big new interstate highway under construction. And the King feels *strongly* about this project. He *insists* on its completion. We hear *urgency* in his voice.

What is it that moves him so deeply? He wants *us*. He wants us free to come back home, with nothing getting in our way: "Remove every obstruction from my people's way." He wants the road back into his heart made obvious and easy to follow—no blind curves, no bumps, no potholes, no speed traps.

"Prepare the way" is our King commanding all his ministers everywhere, "Company's coming, y'all! Make it easy for them to come on in. Sweep away every obstacle, right down to the pebble that might trip up a skateboarder." Did you know God feels that way about you? "Remove every obstruction from my people's way" is like saying, "Toss out every religious complication! Get back to basics! My injured people need it *simple*."

The Protestant Reformers—Martin Luther, Thomas Cranmer, John Calvin—did exactly that. They were a back-to-basics force in history, clearing away the barriers of man-made add-ons to Jesus. And they helped generations of rock-bottom sinners stumble home to God. Now it's our turn, in our time, to keep the gospel accessible to the defeated and despairing.

I'll make it personal. When I realize I've sinned and my conscience is scolding me, in that moment of anxiety and regret I can turn back to Jesus in one of two ways. I can use the direct route, or I can try the roundabout route—which leads nowhere.

Here's the roundabout route. My guilty conscience says, "I've sinned—again! And I hate myself for it. God must hate me too. In fact, he *should* hate me. But if I beat myself up first, if I shame myself and punish myself enough, I might make myself a little more forgivable to God."

But that whole mentality is one of the barriers God wants removed! That strategy for coping doesn't *work*. Our very efforts to make ourselves more presentable only add another layer of sin on top of the sin we committed in the first place. *Everything* about us is mixed with sin. If evil were color-coded, like yellow police tape at a crime scene, then *everything about us at all levels* would glow yellow—including our attempts at proving to God that this time we're serious, this time we really mean it. Our groveling is why verse 14 is here. God lovingly invites us to come now, *as we are*, and just collapse in his arms, *even with all our mess.*

That leaves us with the direct route back to the Lord. We really can hurry *straight* home—through the finished work of Christ on the cross. The prodigal son stumbled home still smelling like the pigsty he'd been wallowing in. But his father was too happy to care (Luke 15:11–32). He threw his arms around that kid. Our self-invented goodness and our self-deceived "not-*so*-badness"—all that ridiculousness holds us back. The only real barrier between us and the embrace of our Father is our hesitancy to come.

In 1759 Joseph Hart told his own story through his great hymn:

Come, ye sinners, poor and needy,
Weak and wounded, sick and sore;
Jesus ready stands to save you,
Full of pity, love and power.

Come, ye weary, heavy-laden,
Lost and ruined by the fall;
If you tarry till you're better,
You will never come at all.

Let not conscience make you linger,
Nor of fitness fondly dream;
All the fitness He requireth
Is to feel your need of Him.[4]

That freedom to get up and come—Isaiah 57:14 takes us there. God has built up and prepared the way. He has removed every obstruction through Christ. John Gerstner explains:

The way to God is wide open. There is nothing standing between the sinner and his God. He has immediate and unimpeded access to the Savior. There is nothing to hinder. No sin can hold him back, because God offers justification to the ungodly. Nothing now stands between the sinner and God but the sinner's "good works." Nothing can keep him from Christ but his delusion that he does not need Him—that he has good works of his own that can satisfy God. . . . All they need is need. All they must have is nothing. . . . But, alas, sinners cannot part with their "virtues." They have none that are not imaginary, but they are real to them. So grace becomes unreal. The real grace of God they spurn in order to hold on to the illusory virtues of

4 Joseph Hart, "Come, Ye Sinners, Poor and Needy" (1759), *The Church Hymnary: Revised Edition* (London: Oxford University Press, 1927), no. 393.

their own. Their eyes fixed on a mirage, they will not drink real water. They die of thirst with water all about them.[5]

How crazy are we to ever think we can be good enough for God! The truth is, our only hope is to be bad enough for God. When we do feel that our good works might have buying power with him, verse 14 restores our sanity: "Remove *every* obstruction from my people's way."

Now let's circle back to that word "for" at the beginning of verse 15. Looking at verses 14 and 15 together, we see how "for" links them. God welcomes us sinners with his amazing grace (v. 14), *for* or *because* that's just who the high and holy one is (v. 15). *God invites us back, fallen all the way to rock bottom, just by being true to himself, not lowering his standards at all.* He really is that merciful.

Let's dare to believe it. After all, Jesus said, "Come to me, all who labor and are heavy laden, and I will give you rest" (Matt. 11:28). And he hasn't withdrawn his grace—not even in your case.

The whole Bible can be summed up in three sentences. God is saying: "I loved you. But I lost you. And I want you back."[6]

5   John H. Gerstner, *Theology for Everyman* (Chicago: Moody Press, 1965), 72–73.
6   It was Tim Keller who suggested this summary years ago. I cannot remember where.

And when our consciences are insisting that we pay at least something for the sins we've committed, now we see what's really going on. Any voice in our heads that puts God off at a distance, with his arms folded and a scowl on his face—that voice is the devil talking.

I love how Martin Luther taught us to fight back:

> When the devil tells us we are sinners and therefore damned, we may answer, "Because you say I am a sinner, I will be righteous and saved." Then the devil will say, "No, you will be damned." And I will reply, "No, for I fly to Christ, who has given himself for my sins. Satan, you will not prevail against me when you try to terrify me by telling me how great my sins are and try to reduce me to heaviness, distrust, despair, hatred, contempt and blasphemy. On the contrary, when you say I am a sinner, you give me armor and weapons against yourself, so that I can cut your throat with your own sword and tread you under my feet, for Christ died for sinners. . . . It is on his shoulders, not mine, that all my sins lie. . . . So when you say I am a sinner, you do not terrify me, but you comfort me immeasurably."[7]

7 Martin Luther, *Galatians*, ed. Alister McGrath and J. I. Packer (Wheaton, IL: Crossway, 1998), 40–41.

Let's believe the gospel. Let's go back to God. Let's keep going back to God. He isn't demanding that we deserve him; he's inviting us to receive him.

Trusting Jesus, Facing Ourselves

Chapter 2 was about betrayal. Somebody violates our trust and breaks our hearts. But in our devastation—God dwells right there. We are not godforsaken, not for one moment.

This chapter is about the opposite of betrayal. Let's think now about our own sins and lies and hypocrisies. Let's face into how we have let others down, how we have broken covenant—and even broken their hearts.

It's hard to think about. The memories are painful—those moments when we were selfish, reckless, stupid. We all know what it's like to realize, "My life was boring and confining. I felt like I deserved better. So I looked at that sin and thought, 'That might be fun.' But now? The bitter aftertaste of shame and self-hatred and devastated relationships! Still worse, I hate this wretched sin, but I also need it. *How do I get free again?*" Our ugly secret sits there deep inside us, like a squatter occupying a building. We're smiling on the outside, but we're sick on the inside. "What if my family, what if my friends, find out?"

Is there any rock bottom as horrible as that?

At this point, some voices will be very ready to yell at us, "Shape up, you sorry loser! If you'll get yourself together, all this will go away!" Really? It's that simple? Maybe you've read the poem "If—," by Rudyard Kipling. It goes like this:

If you can meet with Triumph and Disaster
    And treat those two impostors just the same; . . .

If you can fill the unforgiving minute
    With sixty seconds' worth of distance run,
Yours is the Earth and everything that's in it,
    And—which is more—you'll be a Man, my son![8]

But if we grow strong simply by a rational decision, backed up with enough willpower, why did Jesus say, "Everyone who practices sin is a *slave* to sin" (John 8:34)? *How* can we keep choosing what is good when there is a wild *drivenness* inside us for what is bad? That is *slavery*— our slavery.

So to God we turn, with nothing but need. I remember, back in college, my dad writing a magazine article for us

---

8   Rudyard Kipling, "If—," Poetry Foundation, https://www.poetryfoundation.org/.

students. It was about prayer. The title alone described prayer in a way I'll never forget: "Go to God, and hang on!"[9] In the article, Dad told this story:

A minister preaching at a rescue mission on Skid Row was quoting Kipling's poem "If." When he came to the lines, "If you can fill the unforgiving minute with sixty seconds' worth of distance run . . . ," a desperate voice from the back row shouted, "But what if I can't?"

We understand. But the people up in their self-righteous mushy middle—they have it together enough, or they *think* they do, to look down on Skid Row drunks and all the rest of us. Thing is, Jesus dwells down among *the lowest of the low*. At his cross, our shameful addictions, our embarrassing slavery—everything we hate about ourselves—he took onto himself. It sank him down to death, so that we can get free and live again. No wonder the Bible calls him "a friend of . . . sinners" (Matt. 11:19).

With the grace of Jesus as our only confidence, we can now face ourselves honestly. Let's think it through in three steps.

9 Raymond Ortlund, "Go to God, and Hang On!," *HIS Magazine*, February 1968, 30.

What Is Sin?

Sin is not breaking a petty taboo or overstepping a mere tradition. Sin violates the sacred covenant God made with us. Sin also tears down the beautiful solidarity he built among us.

For example, in Psalm 51, David's prayer of repentance, he uses three words to describe his sin with utter realism:

Have mercy on me, O God,
   according to your steadfast love;
according to your abundant mercy
   blot out *my transgressions*.
Wash me thoroughly from *my iniquity*,
   and cleanse me from *my sin*! (vv. 1–2)

First, "transgression." That is, willful, open-eyed, deliberate revolt against God. David knew exactly what he doing when he took another man's wife and got her pregnant (2 Sam. 11). He *defied* God. His behavior was like giving God the finger. This is the same word used for Joseph's brothers deliberately selling him out (Gen. 50:17). It wasn't a mere mistake.

What on earth was David thinking? Maybe he was feeling confined by his life of obeying God. Maybe he was feeling sorry for himself, like God owed him. Maybe he started thinking, "Why not break free and explore my options?" Restless self-pity gets us doing *horrendous* things.

Second, "iniquity." That is, a warped, twisted, destructive act. This word appears in Isaiah 24:1, where the Lord "will twist" the earth's surface into an unnatural form. The English word *iniquity* sounds quaint, old-fashioned. But think of Gollum, that weird little villain in *The Lord of the Rings*. He wasn't himself anymore. He had descended into something bizarre. Like Gollum, David distorted and degraded his God-given sexuality from life-giving to life-taking, from noble to repulsive.

Iniquity is like taking a smartphone—brilliant communications technology—and using it to hammer nails. That isn't what a smartphone is *for*. It will break.

Third, "sin." That is, missing the mark or losing one's way. This word appears in Judges 20:16, where some highly skilled men could sling a stone "and not miss." We too miss when the map says, "To get home, turn right here." But we think, "I know a better way," and we turn left. No surprise, then, that we get lost, waste time, show up late, disappoint others, and more. Sin is like trying to get healthy eating junk food. It *can't* work. Sin can only miss out and let us down. We end up lost, isolated, depressed—and too proud to admit it.

David sums it up in Psalm 51:4: "[I have] done what is *evil* in your sight." "Evil" is a strong word! Can we be honest enough to use that word to describe things we have done, not just what other people have done?

In each kind of wrong—defying God, misusing his gifts, veering off from his path—we end up in the same low place, with losses and injuries and sadness we didn't foresee. On his thirty-sixth birthday, the brilliant Lord Byron, still a young man, wrote this:

> My days are in the yellow leaf;
>   The flowers and fruits of love are gone;
> The worm, the canker, and the grief
>   Are mine alone![10]

It's not as though, if we just sin more cleverly, we can avoid those painful outcomes. No, sin *always* entraps us in consequences that leave us defeated and shamed. Then our tears flow. Rock bottom, for sure!

How Does God Feel about Us Now?

Does God look at sinners like us with disgust? Why shouldn't he? Look at what we've done—or left undone! What hope do people like us have by now?

10 Lord Byron, "On This Day I Complete My Thirty-Sixth Year," PoetryVerse, https://www.poetryverse.com/.

The Bible shows us the heart of God for sinners like us, who don't deserve God. Check this out:

How can I give you up, O Ephraim?
    How can I hand you over, O Israel? . . .
My heart recoils within me;
    my compassion grows warm and tender. . . .
For I am God and not a man,
    the Holy One in your midst. (Hos. 11:8–9)

God is agonizing over his people. What grieves his heart, more than their sins against him, is the thought of not having them as his people. "How can I give you up?" is his way of saying, "I could *never* give you up!" To God, breaking covenant with us is *unthinkable*, even when we hurt him. And he feels such tender compassion, not because he's bending his rules, but precisely because he is God: "For I am God and not a man." In other words, "I am *not* touchy and explosive and vindictive, like you. I am the Holy One. I am upholding all that it means for me to be *God*, right in your midst. The door to your better future opens here: my endless capacity to love you."[11]

11 Cf. Bruce K. Waltke, *An Old Testament Theology: An Exegetical, Canonical, and Thematic Approach* (Grand Rapids, MI: Zondervan, 2007), 836.

Behold, the God of grace!

And don't tell him he's wrong to be so kind. His grace does not need your correction. You need to accept his grace and stop keeping your distance and run to him and fall into his arms. *What are you waiting for?*

The Bible says Jesus is our sympathetic high priest (Heb. 4:15). The Bible says he deals "gently with the ignorant and wayward" (Heb. 5:2). The Bible is clear: God does not *match* our sins with his grace. He *overmatches* our increased sins with his surplus of hyper-grace (Rom. 5:20). His greatest glory is how he responds *dis*proportionately to our sins upon sins with his "grace upon grace" (John 1:16). The whole logical structure of the biblical gospel is summed up in two simple words: "*much more*" (Rom. 5:15, 17). Your worst sin is far overshadowed by his "much more" grace.

Excuse me for being blunt, but you've met your match. You are not such a spectacular sinner that your sin can defeat the Savior. You might as well give in, come out of hiding, and wave the white flag of surrender. What awaits you and me, right down at our lowest rock bottom, is the finished work of Christ on the cross for the undeserving. And we will find such an astonishing hope *nowhere else*.

All we do in response, all we *can* do, is receive his grace with the empty hands of faith—and yes, even the dirty hands of sin.

How Then Do We Get Traction for Living Better?

Forgiven sinners always want more than forgiveness. We *want* to be forgiven, for sure. But we also want to get freed from the sins that dragged us down in the first place. So you and I are asking, "How do I start *new* patterns of living?" There are three parts to the answer—each part filled with hope.

We Need a Miracle

You and I need a miracle. Does that seem like a letdown? Maybe you feel that a miracle could never happen to *you*? But God *specializes* in miracles, and God is *for* you. If you believe in God at all, then you already believe in miracles. After all, you *are* a miracle—a creation by God himself. So am I. We're far from perfect! That's why this chapter matters. And the miracle you need now is the God who made you remaking you.

Why not go ahead and believe he can re-create you deep within? A miracle isn't an impossibility. It is simply a wonder, a marvel, something amazing.[12] Miracles don't violate "the laws of nature." They leap over those so-called laws. A miracle is like an ambulance speeding to someone's rescue with its

12 Suggested by *miraculum*, the Latin origin of our English word *miracle*. See Carlton T. Lewis and Charles Short, *A Latin Dictionary* (Oxford: Clarendon, 1969), 1148.

lights flashing and its siren blaring, and the ordinary vehicles pull over to the side to make room for that ambulance.[13] God's heart is speeding toward you—yes, the trapped you. He *loves* working wonders at rock bottom.

Take Chuck Colson, for example. He was President Richard Nixon's "dirty tricks artist."[14] But the law caught up with him for his skullduggery in the Watergate scandal of the 1970s. Colson pleaded guilty to obstruction of justice and went to prison. Here's how he summed up his experience there at rock bottom:

> In one sense I had lost everything—power, prestige, freedom, even my identity. In the summer of 1974, as prisoner number 23226 at Maxwell Federal Prison Camp, I stared at the screen of a small black-and-white television set . . . as President Richard Nixon, whom I had served faithfully for three and a half years, resigned his office. It was one of the most desolate experiences of my life.

---

13 One of my favorite seminary profs, Howard Hendricks, put it this way in class one day. And I love how Jürgen Moltmann said it too: "Jesus' healings are not supernatural miracles in a natural world. They are the only truly 'natural' thing in a world that is unnatural, demonized and wounded." Moltmann, *The Way of Jesus Christ: Christology in Messianic Dimensions* (Minneapolis: Fortress, 1993), 98–99.

14 Michael Dobbs, "Charles Colson, Nixon's 'Dirty Tricks' Man, Dies at 80," *Washington Post*, April 21, 2012, https://www.washingtonpost.com/.

But in another sense I had found everything, all that really matters: a personal relationship with the living God. My life had been dramatically transformed by Jesus Christ.[15]

God worked a miracle in Chuck. *But what did that miracle actually look like?* Colson explains how it started. It was a deep conversation one night with his trusted friend Tom Phillips. Chuck still couldn't let go of his proud exterior. But neither could he ignore Tom's words: "I asked Christ to come into my life and I could feel His presence with me, His peace within me. I could sense His Spirit there with me."[16]

What surprised Chuck was how simple it was: "That's what you mean by accepting Christ—you just ask?" Chuck admitted, "I was moved by Tom's story even though I couldn't imagine how such a miraculous change could take place in such a simple way."

As the conversation continued, Tom read aloud the part of C. S. Lewis's book *Mere Christianity* where Lewis calls pride our worst sin, "the complete anti-God state of mind."[17] With that blunt clarity, Chuck's heart began to crack open.

15 Chuck Colson, *Born Again* (Minneapolis: Chosen, 2008), 11.
16 This quote and the following from Colson are from *Born Again*, 122–29.
17 C. S. Lewis, *Mere Christianity* (New York: Macmillan, 1958), 94: "Unchastity, anger, greed, drunkenness, and all that, are mere fleabites in comparison. It was

Just as a man about to die is supposed to see flash before him, sequence by sequence, the high points of his life, so, as Tom's voice read on that August evening, key events in my life paraded before me as if projected on a screen. Things I hadn't thought about in years—my graduation speech at prep school—being "good enough" for the Marines—my first marriage, into the "right" family—sitting on the Jaycees' dais while civic leader after civic leader praised me as the outstanding young man of Boston—then to the White House—the clawing and straining for status and position—"Mr. Colson, the President is calling—Mr. Colson, the President wants to see you right away."

Chuck finally saw himself. But still, his pride held out. He couldn't admit even to his friend that he needed prayer. So he left Tom's house, walked out to his car, and drove off. But he didn't get far—maybe a hundred yards—when the tears began to flow. He pulled over. He didn't realize he was making room for God's ambulance to come work a miracle in him. It wasn't loud and flashy. It was more like meltdown.

---

through Pride that the devil became the devil. Pride leads to every other vice. It is the complete anti-God state of mind."

I was crying so hard it was like trying to swim underwater. . . . With my face cupped in my hands, head leaning forward against the wheel, I forgot about machismo, about pretenses, about fears of being weak. And as I did, I began to experience a wonderful feeling of being released. . . . Then I prayed my first real prayer: "God, I don't know how to find You, but I'm going to try! I'm not much the way I am now, but somehow I want to give myself to you." I didn't know how to say more, so I repeated over and over the words: *Take me*. . . . I stayed there in the car, wet-eyed, praying, thinking, for perhaps half an hour, alone in the quiet of the dark night. Yet for the first time in my life I was not alone at all.

Just like that. And God is able to free you too from the self-exalting lies that keep you trapped, the lies you haven't even begun to see through. God can help. He *wants* to help. And if you refuse and turn away? *You* creating *a new you* out of *the old you*—you want to put your chips on *that* square? Malcolm Muggeridge, who knew a thing or two about sin, explains where that delusion takes us all:

Walking round St. James's Park I thought intensely of the difference between Tolstoy and St. Augustine.

Tolstoy tried to achieve virtue, and particularly continence, through the exercise of his will. St. Augustine saw that, for Man, there is no virtue without a miracle. Thus St. Augustine's asceticism brought him serenity, and Tolstoy's anguish, conflict and the final collapse of his life into tragic buffoonery.[18]

So the first thing you need is the miraculous touch of God's grace way down deep. Chuck Colson's simple prayer, "Take me," is one God loves to hear and answer. And there is *nothing* in his grace to make you a tragic buffoon. He promises this: "I will put my law within them, and I will write it on their hearts" (Jer. 31:33). Not just outward niceness but inward newness. That's the miracle God offers. Do you mind?

Bring your failure, your wreckage, to him. He can take it. He can even flip it into redemption, so that you shine the most brightly where now you hide the most secretly. Your heartbroken "Take me" is where his wonder-working grace shows up.

That's the first thing you need for a new life—a miracle straight from Christ himself. What comes second is something you do: take a new step of faith. Give up on

18 John Bright-Holmes, ed., *Like It Was: The Diaries of Malcolm Muggeridge* (London: Collins, 1981), 434.

every strategy of self-rescue, and turn to Christ alone. It is so freeing!

We Need Faith

The Heidelberg Catechism of 1563 asks, "How are you right with God?" Here's the answer:

> Only by true faith in Jesus Christ. Even though my conscience accuses me of having grievously sinned against all God's commandments, of never having kept any of them, and even though I am still inclined toward all evil, nevertheless, without my deserving it at all, out of sheer grace, God grants and credits to me the perfect satisfaction, righteousness, and holiness of Christ, as if I had never sinned nor been a sinner, as if I had been as perfectly obedient as Christ was obedient for me. *All I need to do is accept this gift of God with a believing heart.*[19]

John Bunyan, the author of *The Pilgrim's Progress*, described how he finally got free. He started looking to Christ. Notice the exteriority, the out-there-ness, the Someone-Else-ness of the grace Bunyan discovered:

19 *Ecumenical Creeds and Reformed Confessions* (Grand Rapids, MI: Board of Publications of the Christian Reformed Church, 1979), 29. Italics added.

One day as I was passing in the field, and that too with some dashes on my conscience, fearing lest all was still not right, suddenly this sentence fell upon my soul, *Your righteousness is in heaven.* And I thought as well that I saw, with the eyes of my soul, Jesus Christ at God's right hand. There, I say, is my righteousness, so that wherever I was or whatever I was doing, God could not say of me, "John Bunyan lacks my righteousness," for that righteousness is right before Him. I also saw that it was not my good frame of heart that made my righteousness better, nor my bad frame that made my righteousness worse, for my righteousness was Jesus Christ Himself, the same yesterday and today and forever. *Now did my chains fall off my legs indeed. I went home rejoicing for the grace and love of God.* Here I lived for some time, sweetly at peace with God through Christ. Oh, I thought, Christ! Christ! There was nothing but Christ before my eyes.[20]

If what you're really banking on is yourself—well, how's that working for you? Why not switch over to Christ? What do you have to lose?

---

20 John Bunyan, *Grace Abounding to the Chief of Sinners* (Philadelphia: Woodward, 1828), 91–92. Style updated. Italics added.

We Need Friends

You and I need a miracle from above. We also need to put our trust in Christ alone. And the third thing we need is friends.

The Bible describes real friendship, real solidarity, like this: "Therefore, confess your sins to one another and pray for one another, that you may be healed" (James 5:16). So my questions to you are obvious: *To whom do you confess your sins? Who is praying for you? Are you experiencing healing?*

We all make New Year's resolutions—and nothing much changes. But with real friends praying for the real you, God promises healing.

One or two trusted friends are all you need. And they need you. Get together once a week and confess your sins to one another. Tell them, especially, that one enslaving sin you'd rather not admit. Until you open up with radical honesty, you're playing a game. But when you put *that* sin out on the table and your friends pray for you about *that* sin, you start getting free. Dietrich Bonhoeffer explained:

The more isolated a person is, the more destructive will be the power of sin over him. Sin wants to remain unknown. The sin must be brought into the light. It is a hard struggle until the sin is openly admitted. The sinner surrenders; he gives up all his evil. He gives his heart to God, and he finds the forgiveness of all his sin in the fellowship of Jesus Christ and his brother. The expressed, acknowledged sin has lost all its power. It has been revealed and judged as sin. Now the fellowship bears the sin of the brother. He is no longer alone with his evil.[21]

Isn't that fellowship where you want to be? You can have it. All you stand to lose is the false self you project to your friends. But you can come out of hiding. Your friends will welcome you and pray for you. You can keep on confessing your sins, and they will keep on praying for you, and God will keep on healing you. Your friends will come alive too. The high and holy God dwells down among the contrite and lowly, reviving their hearts with healing grace.

Honesty and prayer together *as a new way of life*—that's your future opening up! The sin that you're the most sick of—as long as it keeps you in hiding, it keeps its hooks deep into you. But freedom is calling to you, welcoming you in—through confession and prayer with friends. You'll feel so relieved.

Right now is an excellent time to reach out to those trusted friends.

21 Dietrich Bonhoeffer, *Life Together*, trans. John W. Doberstein (New York: Harper & Row, 1954), 112–13.

And while you're at it, go make some things right with the people you betrayed. The Lord will go with you. He will help you.

Questions for Reflection and Discussion

1. Jesus said, "Everyone who practices sin is *a slave* to sin" (John 8:34). That's serious. What did he understand about us and our sin that we tend not to believe, or don't even *want* to believe?

2. What in Isaiah 57:14 do you find most striking, even surprising? And how can that insight help you at a practical level?

3. How, in your own words, does Isaiah 57:14 enhance our view of God's grace in Isaiah 57:15?

4. When we have sinned and need to return to God, we can take "the roundabout route" or "the direct route." What have those two approaches looked like in your own experience? How does the biblical gospel free you to keep using the direct route back to God?

5. Here's a tough question. What, in your judgment, is the worst sin you have ever committed? And with that regret

eating at you inside, how does the biblical gospel guide you back to God's grace?

6. To whom do you confess your sins? Who knows how you're really doing and what isn't going well deep inside you? Who is praying for you?

7. What prayer do you want to offer God? What do you most need to ask him for right now? He will hear, receive, and answer your prayer.

For thus says the One who is high and lifted up,
*   who inhabits eternity, whose name is Holy:*
"I dwell in the high and holy place,
*   and also with him who is of a contrite and lowly spirit,*
to revive the spirit of the lowly,
*   and to revive the heart of the contrite."*

ISAIAH 57:15

4

Lonely

I REMEMBER LYING IN BED at night as a boy, staring out the window at the leaves on a tree in the moonlight—wondering if I was insane. Our family had moved from rural New York to urban California. For me, it was a move from a relaxed and friendly youth culture to an intense and competitive youth culture. It was bewildering. I wondered, "Why don't the kids at school like me? Maybe I'm crazy. I sure feel crazy. That must be it. That's why they don't like me. I'm not normal."

One Sunday some friends of my parents came over for lunch after church. The husband was a psychiatrist. That scared me. I wondered, "Is he going to notice? Will he discover my secret?" Which really was crazy—but not in a clinical sense. I was just lonely.

Naturally, I was with people every day. But "loneliness is not solitude. Solitude requires being alone, whereas loneliness shows itself most sharply in company with others."[1]

Maybe you're thinking, "Ray, did you talk to your dad about it? He would have helped." He would have! He was a wonderful father. But I was too immature even to think of that. So I just kept on. And it wasn't until high school that I began to think I finally belonged. That felt good. But I wish I'd gotten there years before.

This chapter is about loneliness. It's some of our deepest sadness. But the Lord is right there too. "He leads us by ways we could not have guessed, into situations we never expected, to fulfill purposes we never could have imagined"[2]—even in the loneliness of our busy schedules, our frequent moves, and our lost friendships. But this hard journey is *his* journey for us. He is with us *in our real lives*.

Thus far we've thought about what it's like to be betrayed by others, and what it's like to be trapped in our own sins. But if there is any experience that qualifies as

1 Hannah Arendt, *The Origins of Totalitarianism* (New York: Schocken, 2004), 613.

2 Sinclair B. Ferguson, *Devoted to God: Blueprints for Sanctification* (Edinburgh: Banner of Truth, 2016), 52. I thank my friend Benji Magness for alerting me to this quote.

rock bottom, it's loneliness. We can be so grateful that God assures us,

> I dwell . . .
>> *with* him who is of a contrite and lowly spirit.
>> (Isa. 57:15)

How the Word "with" Matters

David French, writing in *The New York Times*, makes a bold claim: "The longer we march through these anxious, sad and divided times, the more I'm convinced that the bigger story, the story behind the story of our bitter divisions and furious conflicts, is our loss of belonging, our escalating loneliness."[3]

He's right. It's one thing to find ourselves down where we never dreamed we'd go, where devastation is our new reality, with permanently life-altering repercussions—and suddenly our lives look like Berlin in 1945, with bombed-out rubble and smoking ruins. But if, down there, we are *also* friendless, misjudged, stigmatized, unsupported—well, there is a reason the worst punishment is called "solitary confinement." Loneliness is hellish torment.

---

3 David French, "Being There," *New York Times*, September 24, 2023, https://www.nytimes.com/.

But God sees us. God cares about us as we lie in bed at night and stare out the window at the leaves on a tree, wondering why the kids at school don't like us, wondering if we're crazy.

To people like us, the little word "with" is worth a lot: ". . . and also *with* him who is of a contrite and lowly spirit." That word is perfect for lonely people. It declares God's presence, his nearness, his loyalty, his advocacy, his solidarity right where we need him. He isn't off at a distance, detached like the Greek gods up on Mount Olympus. He isn't even with us but holding his nose, looking around for an exit strategy.

Thanks to the atoning blood of Christ and the presence of the Spirit, the high and holy one dwells *with* us, in our midst, even in our mess (Lev. 16:16). Down here at rock bottom, he is bringing *all that he is* to *all that we need.* He could not bear to see us suffering alone. He will never leave us nor forsake us (Heb. 13:5). He keeps saying, "Fear not, for I am with you" (Isa. 41:10).

As we have seen, Isaiah 57:15 is a royal proclamation. The King of kings, the high and holy one, *promises* his presence down with his people in their most extreme need. The scholars writing on Isaiah help us feel the force of our Lord's strong assertion.

Matthew Henry, in the eighteenth century, wrote, "He that dwells in the highest heavens dwells in the lowest hearts, and inhabits sincerity as surely as he inhabits eternity. In these he delights."[4] Franz Delitzsch, in the nineteenth century, put it beautifully:

> The Holy One is also the Merciful One. . . . The heaven of heavens is not too great for him, and a human heart is not too small for him to dwell in. He who dwells among the praises of the seraphim does not scorn to dwell among the sighs of a poor human soul.[5]

My friend John Oswalt, writing in the twentieth century, says it this way: "He offers life to those from whom the life has been all but crushed out; he offers life to those whose spirit has been ground down to nothing. They need not be captive to their sin and shame."[6]

Our tenderhearted King knows that being *alone* at rock bottom is unspeakably painful. He has a vivid personal

---

4 Matthew Henry, *Matthew Henry's Commentary on the Whole Bible*, vol. 4, *Isaiah to Malachi* (McLean, VA: MacDonald, 1985), 332.

5 C. F. Keil and F. Delitzsch, *Commentary on the Old Testament*, vol. 7, *Isaiah* (Grand Rapids, MI: Eerdmans, 1969), 379.

6 John N. Oswalt, *The Book of Isaiah: Chapters 40–66* (Grand Rapids, MI: Eerdmans, 1998), 488.

memory of it from that day on his cross when he said, "My God, my God, why have you forsaken me?" (Matt. 27:46). He understands. That's why it's so important to *him* to stay *with* us.

Not everyone does stick around. Some people we thought were friends just aren't there for us, when everything is on the line. And that's when rock bottom is more than just sad. It's terrifying. To be discarded and forgotten, canceled and deleted—our sense of worth shatters. We realize, "They never *were* my friends. I never understood what was really going on. How could I have been so blind?" Yet all the while, their happy parade continues moving on down the street, the trumpets blaring and the drums beating, as if we never even existed. Because we didn't. Not to them. Not really. And then we think, "I won't make that mistake twice!" We withdraw into ourselves. It feels safe. But in truth, the word for that feeling is *temptation*. We are being tempted to shut *God* out.

What Is a Friend?

So let's back up and ask, What is a *real* friend? Answer: an honest-to-goodness friend is *all in*.

Historian Donald Miller explains the strong bonds of comradeship among the American airmen fighting during World War II. It wasn't hatred for the enemy but love for one another that forged their solidarity. Here is a real-life example from a bomber crew:

> Before going into combat, the four sergeants made a pact that if one of them got into a tight spot the others would not abandon him, "no matter what." Weeks later, when their plane was shredded by flak, the pilot ordered everyone to bail out. The top turret gunner, who had not entered the pact, parachuted out of the plane and later reported what happened before he jumped. Enemy shrapnel had jammed the release mechanism of the ball turret, trapping the gunner in his Plexiglas bubble. Unable to extricate him, the other three gunners, all of them uninjured, told their trapped friend that they would die with him. And they did.[7]

True friendship is not a cost-benefit calculation. It is personal commitment, even when everything falls apart—especially when everything falls apart. Isn't that the *best* part of friendship? We might forget that happy Fourth of July cookout with friends last year. But we will *never* forget the

---

7   Donald L. Miller, *Masters of the Air: America's Bomber Boys Who Fought the Air War against Nazi Germany* (New York: Simon & Schuster, 2006), 135. I thank Fr. Bryan White for sharing this with me.

night they rushed to the hospital after our terrible car wreck, how they stayed with us through the ordeal. *And God is like that.* He is all in with you, as your closest friend, at all times.

If God liked you *except when your life implodes*, then God would be one of those false friends who walk away when staying true to you starts costing them. But God is steady, loyal, faithful. The Bible even says he *abounds* in "steadfast love and faithfulness" (Ex. 34:6). He is like "Old Faithful" at Yellowstone National Park, gushing with affection for you. He is like the surf off the coast of Southern California, where I grew up. I can still see those waves rolling in 24/7, sent from storms thousands of miles away and from earth tremors down at the ocean's floor. We didn't cause those waves. All we did was surf them. And God's heart moves that way toward you. You don't cause his love. Your part is to enjoy his love. He is *with* the lowly and the contrite, and he is with you.

Yes, rock bottom is not where we ever wanted to go. But it can be hard to find Jesus anywhere else.

> For though the LORD is high, he regards the lowly,
>   but the haughty he knows from afar. (Ps. 138:6)

Another translation reads, "but he keeps his distance from the proud" (NLT). Thank you, Rock Bottom, for shattering our pride and opening our hearts to Jesus. Malcolm Muggeridge vividly described that kind of moment:

In the gathering darkness every glimmer of light has finally flickered out, it's then that Christ's hand reaches out sure and firm. Then Christ's words bring their inexpressible comfort, then his light shines brightest, abolishing the darkness forever.[8]

It gets even better. By the grace of Christ, others around you will also prove to be true friends. They will be his gift to you, and you to them. *Their* presence with you will bring *his* presence to you.

This is why Shakespeare wisely counseled us,

Those friends thou hast, and their adoption tried, grapple them unto thy soul with hoops of steel![9]

Never let go of your friends—including Christ. Your faith will be mixed with doubts at times. Whose isn't? But as you

8 Malcolm Muggeridge, *The End of Christendom* (Grand Rapids, MI: Eerdmans, 1980), 56.

9 William Shakespeare, *Hamlet*, ed. Roma Gill (Oxford: Oxford University Press, 1992), act 1, scene 3, lines 62–63.

lose some false beliefs along the way, *don't lose Christ too.* Grapple him, and your other true friends, to your soul with hoops of steel!

Our Lonely World Today Is Not Normal

So, back to our topic: loneliness. One of the ironies of our times is how "connected" we are and simultaneously how lonely we are. Let's not assume that our moment in time is an improvement on the past. Let's not assume that our world today is even normal.

Jani and I lived in Scotland in the 1980s. The headmaster of our children's school had grown up on a remote island off the west coast of Scotland back in the 1950s. Only a few hundred people lived on that island. He described it to me one day—how the people *had* to stick together in order just to survive.

For example, every morning the men would do chores on their own crofts. Then at eleven they would meet in the church for "Parliament," where together they decided what they would do with the rest of their workday. They might shear sheep or harvest a crop or fish out at sea. But they worked *together.* They literally could not launch their fishing boats from the beach out into the ocean and then return them onto the beach without helping each other.

After work, they spent their evenings visiting one another in their homes, walking from house to house to enjoy conversation. No one locked their doors. They didn't even knock. They'd open the door, stick their heads in and say, "Hello, we're here!" The whole island was a big family. Friends and neighbors would come in and take a seat and sip whiskey and enjoy a good talk right through the evening. Many of the men had served in the Royal Navy and had seen the world. They had plenty of stories to tell. They weren't boring!

But the headmaster also explained, with sadness, that in the 1960s that beautiful pattern of community faded away. I asked him why. He said, "TV came to the island." Technology weakened community. Screens replaced people. Actors posed as friends. Scripts suppressed conversations.

My point is this: The rich human community those islanders long enjoyed was *normal*. It might seem like a fairy tale to us. But it was real. And God created us to walk through life as faithful friends who stick together in real community.

Today rich human community is desirable—of course. But it also feels optional. We're so busy, and so tired. But let's not normalize our crazy world of today. Let's not feel at home where we have no home. My hunch is, the people on that remote Scottish island experienced less loneliness than we do today in our modern cities with all their outward advantages. It gets me wondering. Which culture is more advanced—ours or theirs?

Where—and Why—We Can Finally Belong

In all our world today, *a healthy church* is one of the few places left where human community can still flourish in rich abundance. Think about that. "Church" isn't one more item on our weekend to-do list. It is an island of humanness in a sea of loneliness. It is *God's* provision for us. It is a major way he cares for us in our suffering.

I quoted David French's article "Being There" earlier. In it he reports that, between 1990 and 2021, the percentage of Americans who say they have no close friends quadrupled. Men especially tend to be lonely. But all of us, men and women—we just don't *belong* the way we used to. And down at rock bottom, we *really* need community. Then we can start feeling less crazy, get our bearings, and begin again—with hope.

Here's the surprising reason a gospel-rich church is a great place for your new beginning: *the doctrine of justification by faith alone*. And I know those words might not leap off the page at you! But I'm serious. Here's why.

Justification by faith—it's *central* to the Bible's message—means that God reinstates us in his favor not because we earn it but because Jesus earned it for us. We stop trying to get God's attention, proving ourselves to him, persuading him. We give up on our strengths and attainments. We finally see that trying to buy God's approval is like using Monopoly money in a real-world economy. All we do, all we *can* do, is receive, with the empty hands of faith, what Jesus is worth. Then, instantly, we're back in good standing with God, as if we had never even sinned. Such grace! And that's justification by faith.

Here is why justification by faith matters to us lonely people. This doctrine does not hang in midair as a bare abstraction. *It creates a new experience of community here among us.* We all come in the same way—with the empty hands of faith, which God fills with the rich merit of Christ. Our shared grace is why the Bible says, "Therefore welcome one another as Christ has welcomed you" (Rom. 15:7). The welcoming heart of Jesus creates a welcoming heart toward one another. So, my brokenhearted friend, welcome! You belong—yes, *you*! You belong as much as I do. Jesus says so. Yes, we may be at rock bottom. But we sure don't have to be lonely down here.

His grace bringing us *in*—and not the spiffy us but the embarrassed us—his grace gathers together a ragtag band of surprised, grateful, hopeful sinners. Under the covering of justification by faith, equally shared, we enter real community. Would we want to be anywhere else? God's grace rules nowhere else.

But justification *by works* destroys community. Navigating reality by clawing our way upward, proving our superiority, we inevitably step on people and stoke the fires of resentment in return. And isn't that our world today—a merciless meltdown? It intensifies loneliness.

Jesus saw our merciless comparisons in his own time. It grieved him. He told a story about it "to some who trusted in themselves that they were righteous, and treated others with contempt" (Luke 18:9). Those two dynamics always go together—trusting in our own righteousness and treating others with contempt. It's when we look at someone else and think, "Well, I might not be perfect, but I've never sunk *that* low!"

In fact, the phrase translated "treated others with contempt" can be paraphrased "nothing-ized others."[10] That is, "You don't count. You might as well not even exist—not in my world. So I will ignore you and keep chasing my self-idealizing dreams." No wonder loneliness is spiking. Self-justification is all about shaming the unworthy, excluding the unwashed.[11]

10 This line of thought is suggested by A. T. Robertson, *Word Pictures in the New Testament*, vol. 2, *Luke* (Nashville: Broadman, 1930), 232.

11 C. S. Lewis analyzes the poisonous recipe of this cocktail in his essay "The Inner Ring," in *The Weight of Glory and Other Addresses* (Grand Rapids, MI: Eerdmans, 1974), 55–66.

But in a healthy church, how different our experience is! We walk in and sense the difference immediately. The vibe, the tone, the atmosphere—it's honest, merciful, relaxed, encouraging. Why? Because everyone comes in on the same terms—not the clenched fists of demand, but the empty hands of faith. Justification by faith means there is no elite riding up in first class, with prior boarding and extra leg room, while the ordinary folks are crammed back in the coach section. *Everyone* is in first class, flying home by God's grace in Christ. That *doctrine* of grace creates a *culture* of grace: "Therefore welcome one another, as Christ has welcomed you" (Rom. 15:7). Welcome, friend.

Our hyper-individualistic culture doesn't understand. It pressures us to "be true to ourselves." Can we see how bizarre that is? How can George McFly flourish under the frown of Biff Tannen?[12] How can we "be true to ourselves" while being indoctrinated by the fashionable intimidation of our culture? As one man put it, "Can you remember who you were, before the world told you who you should be?"[13] That's why a healthy church is such a relief. It's an oasis of gentle belonging. We can come in, let our guard down, and rest for a while. Jesus

---

12 As in *Back to the Future*, the 1985 movie.

13 Often attributed to Charles Bukowski, though I have been unable to confirm its source.

himself creates it by his doctrine of justification by faith alone. *He* welcomes us, and he makes the rules!

Here's a suggestion for practical follow-through. Whenever we believers get together, let's not be looking at our phones. Let's put them away and keep them away, to show respect for one another and be as present and attentive as we can be. Our moments together are precious. We'll never get them back again.

Recently I received an email from my cell phone provider with this pitch: "Stay connected on more devices!" *Really?* They think that's what I *want?* I don't even like the word *connect*—not when it comes to people. If I jump-start the dead battery in my car, I *connect* the jumper cables to the battery terminals. But when I shake hands with a friend, that's *personal touch.* It is sacred, glorious, human. Onlineland is a bubble of imaginary relationships, keeping us lonely people far from real, life-giving experience together. Let's not be fooled.

The apostle John wrote, "I would rather not write with pen and ink. I hope to see you soon, and we will talk face to face" (3 John 13–14). If John were living today, my hunch is that he'd use a basic flip phone and spend more time enjoying coffee with friends at Starbucks. And our sad world would suffer less loneliness.

You Are Never Abandoned

Jesus looks his followers right in the eye and says, "You are my friends" (John 15:14). If you belong to him, he has welcomed you into his circle of intimates. You might feel lonely, but you are not *alone*. So let's say that an angel in heaven asks our Lord above, "Sir, who are some of your friends down there?" Do you realize that *your name* might well be the first one he mentions? He cherishes *you* as a personal friend. You're in his contacts. He knew in advance what you would cost him, but he doesn't resent you for it. He's too happy for that. He is overjoyed just to have you close.

But if you haven't become definite about following Jesus, now is the time. He is inviting *you* in. If you feel you've sinned too horribly for him to want you around, consider this. Benjamin Grosvenor, in a sermon preached over two hundred years ago, imagined out loud what Jesus and his apostles might have talked about as the Lord was sending them out to evangelize the world. For example, what if they run across that Roman soldier who pierced Jesus's side with his spear (John 19:34)? Grosvenor pictured Jesus saying this:

If you meet that poor wretch who thrust the spear into my side, tell him there is another way, a better way, to get to my heart. . . . I will cherish him in that very heart he has wounded. He will find the blood he shed an ample atonement for the sin of shedding it. And tell him for me, he will cause me more pain by refusing this offer of my blood, than when he drew my blood forth.[14]

Have you hurt Jesus deeply? I have too. But that doesn't change how he feels about you. He could not love you more. You can safely come to him as you are. He will welcome you and befriend you. You will finally *belong*. And if you do turn away, his parade doesn't keep moving on down the street, as if you don't matter. No, he stops, and he waits— longingly. And when you do turn and come to him, that's when his party *really* rocks—out of his sheer joy to have *you* there. *Why wait?*

And the longer you follow Jesus, the less lonely you will feel. He will stick with you. He will never turn on you, or trade you in for someone better, or get tired of you, or even get a job transfer and move out of town and find new friends because he's gotten too busy. Jesus is right here, right now, *for you*, with all his heart. And he's not going away.

14 Benjamin Grosvenor, *Sermons by Benjamin Grosvenor*, ed. John Davies (Isle of Wight: Williams and Smith, 1808), 8. Style updated.

So let's not give up on one another either. So much is at stake in our solidarity. The Bible says *"we are members of one another"* (Eph. 4:25). Which means I can't be myself without you! And let's be clear. We are *not* like the "members" of a country club, but we *are* like the members of a human body—arms and legs, eyes and ears (1 Cor. 12:12–27). You and I find our identity and happiness and vitality not in isolation by ourselves but in close touch with one another. And our very differences can make us feel more alive.

The Bible speaks of "bearing" with others, patiently absorbing what rubs us the wrong way. How could it be otherwise? Jesus "bore the sin of many" (Isa. 53:12). No surprise, then, that the Bible says, "Bear one another's burdens, and so fulfill the law of Christ" (Gal. 6:2). He is why we hang in there and put up with one another. If we didn't belong to him, we sure wouldn't be that merciful. Our relationships would be predatory. But now, with Jesus, our relationships start looking more like him—cruciform. Dietrich Bonhoeffer understood how great it can be. "Bearing" includes accepting another person's

weaknesses and oddities, which are such a trial to our patience, everything that produces frictions, conflicts and collisions among us. To bear the burden of the other person means involvement with the created reality of the other, to accept and affirm it, and, in bearing with it, to break through to the point where we take joy in it.[15]

I love that. When I get past my own selfishness, I can start finding my friend's quirks downright lovable. That's a breakthrough.

The early Christian church dared to embody that beautiful community. And the watching world did not respond with, "But of course. Everyone is like that." Far from it. They *marveled* at the early Christians, "How they love one another! How they are ready to die for one another!"[16] After all, didn't Jesus say, "I came to cast *fire* on the earth" (Luke 12:49)? His love is how we burn brightly together, by his grace, for his glory. In *The Incendiary Fellowship*, Elton Trueblood shows how spiritual underachievers, like us, can experience that miracle:

As everyone knows, it is almost impossible to create a fire with one log, even if it is a sound one, while several poor logs may make an excellent fire if they stay together as they

15 Dietrich Bonhoeffer, *Life Together*, trans. John W. Doberstein (New York: Harper & Row, 1954), 101.

16 Tertullian, *The Apology of Tertullian*, ed. H. A. Woodham (Cambridge: Cambridge University Press, 1843), 132.

burn. The miracle of the early Church was that of poor sticks making a grand conflagration.[17]

We can be the poor logs we really are. But if we'll stay together as we burn, the world around will feel the warmth. They will see that Jesus really is here among us, and many will come join us. So, sign me up! You too?

In our burning fire—a healthy church community—everyone matters. Everyone can give life. A persecuted Chinese Christian said it well:

Units have no special use, exercise no ministry, can easily be overlooked or left out. . . . But members are otherwise. They cannot be passive in the Body; they dare not merely stand by looking on. . . . We cannot say, "I don't count." We dare not attend meetings merely as passengers, while others do the work. We are His Body, and members in particular, and it is when all the members fulfill their ministry that the life flows.[18]

Together we flourish—with tears and laughter, failures and successes. *And loneliness hightails it out of there!*

17 Elton Trueblood, *The Incendiary Fellowship* (New York: Harper & Row, 1967), 107.
18 Watchman Nee, *What Shall This Man Do?* (Fort Washington, PA: CLC, 1961), 113.

It's Time to Come Together

Our loneliness is a sorrow God never meant us to bear. Let's tear down every self-created wall of isolation. Let's break free from our little worlds of fear and resentment. Christ has made us his very body. Let's grapple one another to our souls *with hoops of steel.*

If right now you are at a threshold where something new is very near, C. S. Lewis might nudge you closer: "Friendship is unnecessary, like philosophy, like art, like the universe itself (for God did not need to create). It has no survival value; rather, it is one of those things which give value to survival."[19]

For me, Bishop J. C. Ryle seals the deal. He helps me see the obvious I don't want to miss out on: "This world is full of sorrow because it is full of sin. It is a dark place. It is a lonely place. It is a disappointing place. The brightest sunbeam in it is a friend. *Friendship halves our troubles and doubles our joys.*"[20]

How then can we cross the threshold and enter deeply into faithful friendships? Here are two steps.

One, fill your loneliness for Jesus with Jesus. Your friends can't be what only he is. Why not let your friends be imperfect and wonderful while you lean into Jesus as perfect and

19 C. S. Lewis, *The Four Loves* (New York: Harcourt, Brace, Jovanovich, 1960), 103.
20 John Charles Ryle, *Practical Religion*, ed. J. I. Packer (London: James Clarke, 1959), 221. Italics added.

wonderful? Then you'll be ready for some really great friends, who don't have to be perfect.

Two, live dangerously, and give your heart away. And those *are* the alternatives: either staying safe in your loneliness or defying your fear. Why not stick your neck out and take a chance? If Jesus has made you a member of his church body, then dare to believe it and take the plunge with one or two trustworthy Christian friends. Meet with them. Share your feelings. David and Jonathan even formed a covenant of friendship together (1 Sam. 18:1–4). They defined what their solidarity would look like. You and your friends can do the same, if that would help. Dream out loud together about the friendship you all long for. Then funnel down to glad agreement on the new patterns of support that can strengthen all of you. Your loneliness will never, in this life, go away completely. But you can be a profound friend to other believers, and you and they will feel more alive than ever before.

You can be impressive, or you can be known, but you can't be both. Why not get close to your friends in Christ, and all of you together become known? God himself will dwell there among you.

So, go kick your loneliness right in the teeth—and have fun doing it!

Questions for Reflection and Discussion

1. When in your life have you found yourself friendless, misjudged, stigmatized, unsupported? What was happening in your circumstances? What was happening within your heart?

2. That small but weighty word "with" in Isaiah 57:15—how does that word, that realization, help you face your reality right now? As your mind and heart "riff" on that word in the verse, list your thoughts and feelings.

3. We live in a universe where ultimate reality is not the laws of physics but the beauty of relationships—starting within the triune God above. How would you describe the beauty you have seen in your truest friends?

4. What stands out to you as you picture the quality of community among those Scottish islanders back in the 1950s? Is there one aspect of their solidarity that you most desire to reproduce within your own world today? If so, which is it? How might you take a next step in that positive direction?

5. How does the doctrine of justification by faith alone lift a church into relational beauty together? As that teaching

gets traction in our hearts, how does it change "the ground rules" with one another at church?

6. David and Jonathan made a covenant together. They resolved to be faithful friends, even when it was hard. With whom might you make such a commitment? List the trustworthy Christian friends near you who might be willing to form that strong bond of friendship in Christ. Why not give them a call and talk it over?

7. What prayer do you want to offer God at this point? What do you most need from him *now*? Go ahead, and ask him for that very blessing which will help you stay steady and keep going.

For thus says the One who is high and lifted up,
   who inhabits eternity, whose name is Holy:
"I dwell in the high and holy place,
   and also with him who is of a contrite and lowly spirit,
to revive the spirit of the lowly,
   and to revive the heart of the contrite."

ISAIAH 57:15

5

Dying

"THE STATISTICS ABOUT DEATH are very impressive," said
the playwright George Bernard Shaw. "One out of one
dies."[1] Both the famous and the unknown, the virtuous
and the vile, the strong and the weak—every one of us
has a birthday, but every one of us also has a deathday. We
know when our birthdays fall on the calendar, but we have
no idea about our deathdays. But that final day is circled
on God's calendar for your life and mine. He knows what
he's doing, and *he's for us*. But we must get ready now,
because it won't be long before we're there. Not long at
all. Your life is like the vaporous breath you exhale on a
cold night. It appears momentarily, but it soon vanishes

---

1   Quoted in "Book Briefs," *Christianity Today*, February 27, 1976.

(James 4:14). Let's think about it *now*, while we still have our wits about us.

We might wonder how it will go down for us on our final day in this world. Maybe it will be cancer, or a car wreck, or war, or murder, or just old age. But unless Jesus comes back first, you *will* die. And there is no deeper rock bottom than the final collapse not just of your career but of your very life itself. Death is the bottom of rock bottom. Death is the underside of the bottom of rock bottom. And that is why the high and holy one will be so present with you at that moment of your death.

The Bible says,

> Precious in the sight of the LORD
>   is the death of his saints. (Ps. 116:15)

The key word is "precious"—the opposite of cheap or throw-away. When you come to die, and you can no longer do your job or provide for your family or serve your church or do anything helpful to anyone, and you cannot earn your way any longer at all—the Lord will not crumple you up and throw you away like a piece of trash. In that moment of utter weakness and need, you will be *precious* to him. He will treasure you, value you, hold on to you. And on that day, so significant to *him*—when that day comes, as it soon will, then the risen Christ will say to you, "Today you will be with me in paradise" (Luke 23:43).

What's more, if our majestic Lord is present with us at our death, and he will be, then he is surely with us in all our sufferings leading up to death. All our dreadful foretastes of death—disease, injury, disability, exhaustion, depression, dementia—he will go with us, as our ally, through every experience that whispers death's steady approach. However weak we become, still "*underneath* are the everlasting arms" (Deut. 33:27). There is no way our Lord will keep his distance from us down in our deepest need. That is the very place where he dwells most intentionally, with newness of life we scarcely believe is real until we experience it for ourselves.

Isaiah 57:15 says that he revives the *spirit* of the lowly and revives the *heart* of the contrite, even as our *bodies* are aging and dying. In fact, our risen Lord is so able to visit us then that the hard part might not be dying. Amazingly, the hard part might be surviving the glory of his felt presence. For example, John Nisbet (1627–1685) was a Scottish martyr for the gospel during what historians call "the Killing Times." Nisbet was held in prison, chained down, condemned to hang. They mistreated his body. But in his spirit, his heart, he was revived by the Lord. Here is what Nisbet said: "It has pleased Him to give me such real impression of unspeakable glory as, without constant and immediate supports from the Giver, will certainly overwhelm me. This frail tabernacle is not able to hold up under what I now feel."

A few days before his hanging, he was experiencing the presence of God so wonderfully that he cried out in prayer, "O for Friday! O for Friday! O Lord, give patience to wait Thy appointed time! O give strength to bear up under Thy sweet, sweet Presence!"[2]

Who wouldn't love to suffer and die that way? Maybe God will give us that privilege. We can ask him.

Final Thoughts from Isaiah 57:15

Isaiah's wondrous declaration has guided us along our journey together. As we have been helped by the insights of other thinkers, maybe you've noticed that I like old books. And the older, the better! For example, the commentary by Campegius Vitringa (1659–1722), the brilliant Dutch scholar,[3] shows

2 Jock Purves, *Fair Sunshine: Character Studies of the Scottish Covenanters* (Edinburgh: Banner of Truth, 1990), 91–92.

3 Franz Delitzsch, in C. F. Keil and F. Delitzsch, *Commentary on the Old Testament*, vol. 7 (Grand Rapids, MI: Eerdmans, 1969), 63, calls Vitringa's work on Isaiah "still incomparably the greatest of all the exegetical works upon the Old Testament." High praise!

us the richness of that repeated verb "revive" in the climactic lines of our verse:

> The prophet twice used the word *revive* because of its remarkable emphasis and appropriateness. . . . It involves every work and every action which the Holy Spirit exerts, in his gracious arrangement, toward restoring the soul of man to wholeness, awakening, encouraging, sanctifying and cheering the soul with a sense of God's favor and presence.[4]

Whatever your need and mine—and we'll have many more needs as we come to the end—the Holy Spirit has a full range of helps and remedies: restoring, awakening, encouraging, sanctifying, and cheering, for starters! They're all packed inside that repeated word "revive."

Let's go further back. John Calvin (1509–1564) was an insightful student of the Bible, to say the least. Sheer genius! Here is Calvin on God's reviving power coming down to the lowly and contrite:

> [God] descends even to the lifeless, that he may breathe new life into them and form them anew. Twice he expressly

4 Campegius Vitringa, *Commentarius in librum prophetiarum Jesaiae*, vol. 2 (Herborn: Andreae, 1722), 760.

mentions the "lowly spirit," and the "contrite heart," that
we may know that these promises belong to those who,
in their afflictions, shall not be hardhearted and rebellious
and who, in short, shall lay aside all arrogance and be meek
and lowly.[5]

God's part is to give life to the lifeless. Our part is to be
dead enough to receive his life-giving touch. God has dynamic
energy. We have exhausted lethargy. The two go really well
together, as long as we don't mind staying low before God.
Thanks for that clarity, John Calvin!

Finally, going even further back, deep into Jewish scholar-
ship from the early centuries AD, Rabbi Alexandri offers this
wisdom: "If an ordinary person should make use of a broken
vessel, it is demeaning to him. But as to the Holy One, blessed
be he, all the vessels that he uses are broken."[6]

God can use broken vessels, and even dying vessels.
What else does he have to work with? So let's trust in
God as we face the unknown future. Our risen Savior is

---

5 John Calvin, *Commentary on the Book of the Prophet Isaiah*, vol. 4, trans. William
Pringle (Grand Rapids, MI: Eerdmans, 1948), 214. I have changed the translation slightly.

6 Quoted in John Goldingay, *Isaiah 56–66: A Critical and Exegetical Commentary*
(London: Bloomsbury, 2014), 139.

already present there, waiting for us with every grace we will need moment by moment. Let's think it through now, with that confidence.

Death Is Not Our Friend

It is sentimental nonsense to think of death as "part of the circle of life"—whatever that means. Simone de Beauvoir rightly asserted, "There is no such thing as a natural death." Bluntly, she called death a "violation."[7] When someone you love dies, they don't just move out of town. You will never be with them again in all this world. A chapter gets ripped out of the story of your life—and maybe a lot more than a chapter. You *feel* the loss. You never *stop* feeling the loss.

The Bible is soberly realistic. Death entered the world *after* God's good creation was completed (Gen. 1–3). Death is not natural. Death invaded and vandalized God's glorious creation through Adam's sin (Rom. 5:12). So we can't be okay with death any more than we can be okay with sin.

The Bible insults death as our "last enemy," to be destroyed by our risen Christ (1 Cor. 15:26). Every day in this world our mighty Savior is destroying his enemies by making them

---

7 Simone de Beauvoir, *A Very Easy Death: A Memoir* (New York: Pantheon, 1985), 106.

his friends—like you and me.[8] But a day is coming when Jesus will raise our bodies, the humblest part of us, these earthy bodies we lug around—he will raise *even our bodies* from death. He will make your body alive again, *better than before*. You will rise immortal, never to die again, never even to get tired. And, thanks to Jesus alone, death itself will die, and "everything sad will come untrue."[9]

Until that happy day, we will continue to suffer. Someday soon you and I will keel over and collapse in death. But we can also know how the heart of Jesus feels for us all along the way. For example, with the other mourners at the tomb of his friend Lazarus, "Jesus *wept*" (John 11:35). He didn't go into denial. He didn't trivialize the moment with a glib "Cheer up, everybody! Lazarus will always be with us—in some sense, sort of, maybe." No, the Bible says, "When Jesus saw [Mary] weeping, and the Jews who had come with her also weeping, *he was deeply moved in his spirit and greatly troubled*" (John 11:33). And his feelings

---

8 When Abraham Lincoln was asked why he seemed conciliatory toward the South, he replied, "Do I not destroy my enemies when I make them my friends?" See F. Kathleen Foley, " 'Lincoln' Seeks to Set the Facts Straight," *Los Angeles Times*, April 3, 1996. https://www.latimes.com/archives/la-xpm-1996-04-03-ca-54372 -story.html.

9 J. R. R. Tolkien, *The Return of the King*, pt. 3 of *The Lord of the Rings* (Boston: Houghton Mifflin, 1994), 930.

didn't change, like a passing wave of emotion. The Bible says that Jesus was "deeply moved *again*" (John 11:38). In fact, another translation of verse 33 reads, "He was moved with indignation" (REB). Still another reads, "A deep anger welled up within him" (NLT).

When Lazarus died, Jesus was more than sad. He was *furious* at death for destroying his friend and breaking the hearts of everyone there. This word translated "deeply moved" was used in secular Greek of a horse snorting.[10] So Jesus was *fuming* at the atrocity that death is. The God of the Bible is opposite to Aristotle's Unmoved Mover, who is "little involved in the world," since we are "beneath such notice."[11] B. B. Warfield, the great Princeton theologian, understood our Lord's tender, angry heart.

Jesus approached the grave of Lazarus in a state not of uncontrollable grief but of irrepressible anger. . . . [The funeral procession] brought poignantly home to his consciousness the evil of death, its unnaturalness, its "violent tyranny" as Calvin phrases it. In Mary's grief, he

---

10 *The Cambridge Greek Lexicon*, ed. James Diggle, 2 vols. (Cambridge: Cambridge University Press, 2021), 1:476.

11 See Raymond C. Ortlund Jr., *Isaiah: God Saves Sinners* (Wheaton, IL: Crossway, 2005), 101.

contemplates the general misery of the whole human race and burns with rage against the oppressor of men. . . . It is death that is the object of his wrath.[12]

So now we know. Jesus *hates* death. He hates *your* death. The death of his friend Lazarus made Jesus furious. He detests the obscenities of death—the pain, the separation, the destruction, the tears of the bereaved, the loss of happy days together, the years of loneliness. He hates death so much he went to that hideous cross to die our final death for us. Thanks to him, we don't have to suffer the second death and eternal hell (Rev. 21:8). Death is our enemy, it is his enemy, and by his resurrection he *defeated* his and our wretched enemy.

So let's be decisive. Here is what *isn't* true. It isn't true that our present existence is life, and we are on our way to some vague, shadowy "*after*-life." Here is what *is* true. Our present existence is a living death, and through Christ we are on our way to *the life that is truly life*—both our souls and our bodies alive with nuclear-powered life forever! Death, our enemy, will win short term. But Jesus our friend has won long term.

12 B. B. Warfield, *The Emotional Life of Our Lord* (Wheaton, IL: Crossway, 2022), 63–66.

We Can Face Death Bravely

I read somewhere that, during the Victorian era of the 1800s, people talked often about death, and sex was their taboo subject. By now we've flipped it. We talk freely about sex, and death is our taboo subject. Even *Christians* shy away from talking about death. But why? Why should we fear *anything*? We are following our risen Lord into a future brimful of *life*.

With Jesus, death is no longer our end. He has made it our *release*. So, Death, you sorry loser, *we will outlive you!* We will dance on your grave forever (Rev. 21:4)! With the poet John Donne, we hurl this defiant taunt at our enemy:

One short sleep past, we wake eternally
And death shall be no more; Death, *thou* shalt die.[13]

But for now, until we're together there in heaven, high-fiving each other and shouting our fool heads off and dancing like teenagers again for the sheer joy of being fully alive forever—for now, two things about facing death. One is obvious, just common sense. The other is not so obvious, but very brave.

13 John Donne, "Death, Be Not Proud," https://www.poetryfoundation.org/.

Obviously, let's fight death every day. We want to live for Christ as long as we can, as vigorously as we can. So, at a practical level, let's take our vitamins, stay active, buy life insurance, make out a will—and not text while we drive! Let's cover every base. With Jesus, we have so much to live for, while we live. But these are obvious steps to take. Let's just not neglect them!

Not so obviously, let's also prepare to die bravely, even magnificently. Here are two insights, from an obscure passage back in the Old Testament, that can help us prevail when our final moment comes.[14] The Bible says that, near the end of Moses's life, God gave him a surprising command: "Go up this mountain . . . and view the land of Canaan, which I am giving to the people of Israel for a possession. And die on the mountain which you go up, and be gathered to your people" (Deut. 32:49–50).

The first insight is this. Your death will be your crowning act of obedience to God. Did you catch God's final command to Moses? "And *die* on the mountain." Moses did obey that command, by God's grace. His death, therefore, was not his pathetic, crushing defeat; it was his final, triumphant obedi-

---

14 Ray Ortlund, "Friend, You Can Be Ready to Die: Two Ways to Prepare Now," Desiring God, October 14, 2022, https://www.desiringgod.org/.

ence. It was even what we call a mountaintop experience: "And die *on the mountain.*"

Yes, death can be painful and humiliating. We should expect that. But we can expect more than misery. If, like Moses, you are God's servant, your death will include a deeper reality. The Lord himself will lead you to and through your dying day, and you will follow him. *You will die obeying Jesus.* It's why you're reading this book right now. You love him, and he loves you. None of us is all that great at living and dying like Christians. But we do mean business with him, as he does with us. And my point is this: on your dying day you will *still* be following him faithfully and obediently. You followed him with a first step, and you will follow him with a last step. And as you think ahead about it, don't worry about failing him at that final moment. He who commands you will also carry you. *And you will glorify God by your death.*

Remember when Jesus predicted Peter's death? The Bible says, "This [Jesus] said to show by what kind of death [Peter] was to glorify God" (John 21:19). Peter didn't *just* die; he *glorified God* by his death. He did this even though he had no control over how he died (John 21:18). And my dear Christian friend, you too will glorify God by your death.

Your part in it all? The Bible answers that question: "And after saying this Jesus said to Peter, 'Follow me'" (John 21:19).

Peter didn't have to orchestrate a dramatic scenario and get the actors in place and rehearse it and make it all happen. All Peter had to do, to die with the glory of God upon his death, was follow Jesus, one day at a time, all the way there. And Jesus is saying the same thing to you today: "Your death will glorify God. How? I'll take care of that. Your part is just to keep following me, step by step. Deal?"

Far from a grandiose human stunt, a God-glorifying death is basically simple. Follow Christ faithfully right now, and he will put his glory upon you then. The angels in heaven above, watching his grace unfold in that poignant moment, will erupt in cheers and shouts and applause. Then they'll go *totally* nuts with joy, a big standing ovation, to see you walking through the pearly gates into heaven above—you, with the biggest grin on your face you've ever shown, your countenance radiant with a happiness that doesn't even exist in this world. Your Lord and Savior, Jesus Christ, will step forward to greet you. You will bow. He will smile. He might even proclaim a special day in your honor there in the Holy City. And the thought might occur to you, "My death? It sure wasn't my end! It didn't even turn out to be a bad day. Thanks to Jesus my King, my death became my doorway to this joy I longed for all those years in the sad world below. My death was the climactic privilege of my entire earthly journey." Released from this life, you will burst into God's presence with off-the-charts happiness.

Look what the Bible says: "All things are *yours*, whether . . . the world or life or *death*" (1 Cor. 3:21–22). Your life is a gift from God. And your death will be a gift from God, opening up everything you most deeply long for.

My dad died of pulmonary fibrosis. In his latter years, his lungs became hardened and leathery and couldn't process oxygen. He felt like he was underwater, fighting for air all the time, especially when he exerted himself. One time back in 2007, in his declining days, at his home in California, he was finding it very hard to catch his breath. Mom found him collapsed on the floor. She was deeply distressed, of course. And between his attempts to gulp down a breath of air, Dad said to her, "No, Anne, no. It's a gift. This is a gift." And several months later, Dad died. On the day of his death, the family gathered around his bed there at the hospital. They read Scripture. They sang hymns. Dad pronounced the Blessing of Aaron over the family (Num. 6:24–26). He bowed his head, and he died, glorifying God.

I don't know, of course, if you and I will have a chance to speak to our families like that when our time comes. But I do know this: we can be *ready* for a God-glorifying death, however he wants it to go down. Our part is to decide now that, by God's grace, as long as we retain mental clarity, *we will worship him*. And when we can no longer string together one cogent thought after another, then *he will carry us*—all the way home.

We prevail over death not by masking its gains with plastic surgeries. We prevail not by putting up a bold front with sheer willpower. In Beethoven's final moments, for example, "he momentarily opened his eyes, lifted his right hand, and clenched it into a fist. When his hand fell back from this effort, Beethoven was dead."[15] But we prevail over death by trusting and praising God right *through* death. He will be glorified. And we will be happy.

Here is a classic summary of this practical Christianity, moment by moment, come what may:

I appeal to you therefore, brothers, by the mercies of God, to present your bodies as a living sacrifice, holy and acceptable to God, which is your spiritual worship. Do not be conformed to this world, but be transformed by the renewal of your mind, that by testing you may discern what is the will of God, what is good and acceptable and perfect. (Rom. 12:1–2)

15 Maynard Solomon, *Beethoven* (New York: Schirmer, 1997), 381.

What's the point here? As our minds are renewed with insights from the gospel, something great happens. We start discovering how good and acceptable and perfect the will of God really is—good and acceptable and perfect *to us*, even as we weaken and die. "No, Anne, no. It's a gift. This is a gift."

Your happiness is no longer limited to the narrowness of a coffin. Your future is as big as the new heavens and the new earth, that eternal place being prepared for you by your risen King (John 14:2–3). Your hope is not petty and small—like living an ideal, designer life here in this world. Here's how big your future is in Christ: "There is more than enough room in my Father's home" (John 14:2 NLT)—room enough for you to live and run free and discover and enjoy *to the max* forever! Your future is a renewed world, with a renewed human race from every tribe, tongue, language, and culture, all gathered together in God's glorious presence, partying like this sad world cannot imagine (Rev. 7:9–12).

Whatever earthly path leads us *there* is fine with us. The more we walk with Christ, the more we find one overruling desire moving our hearts: "that I may know him and the power of his resurrection, and may share his sufferings, becoming like him in his death, that *by any means possible* I may attain the resurrection from the dead" (Phil. 3:10–11). Paul isn't talking about earning his way to heaven. He's signing up for *whatever it takes* to get there. So do we. The *worst* this world can do is send us on to heaven!

Your future is *grandeur*.[16] And it's only a breath away. In fact, given the glory of every believer's eternal future, I've never seen a Christian funeral do justice to the magnitude of the moment. Of course, let's make every Christian funeral as meaningful as we can. A blood-bought sinner has just stepped on Satan's neck and leapt up into eternal happiness, by God's grace, for God's glory! And on the day of your funeral, this uncomprehending world will trudge along in its weary way. But your believing family and friends there at church will understand what's really going on. And they will rejoice—weep and rejoice.

Here is our other insight from the death of Moses. Your death will be your final act of obedience to God in this world. And even more, your death will be your happy meeting with the saints in his better world above. When God commanded Moses to die, he also enriched Moses's expectations of his death: "Die on the mountain which you go up, *and be gathered to your people*" (Deut. 32:50).

16 The following paragraphs draw from Ray Ortlund, "Friend, You Can Be Ready to Die."

To be with our Lord above is the ultimate human experience. But he himself includes in that sacred privilege "the communion of saints," to quote the Apostles' Creed. When you die, you will be "gathered to your people"—all the believers in Jesus who have gone before you into God's immediate presence. They are *your* people. And you will live happily among them forever.

Heaven will not be solitary you with Jesus alone. You will be among countless others surrounding his Throne of Grace, all of you glorifying and enjoying him together with euphoric enthusiasm. Right now, in this world, we are "the church militant"—to use the traditional wording. We're engaged in a mighty conflict. But even now, we are one with "the church triumphant" above. And the moment we die, (to change the metaphor) we round third base and sprint to home plate, to the rowdy cheers of the whole team waiting for us there, as we score our home run.

Think about life together in that shared happiness above. No broken friendships, not even awkward aloofness. We all will be united before Christ in a celebration of his salvation too joyous for any selfishness to sneak into our hearts. Grievance will vanish. Embarrassment will melt away. Tenderness and respect will set the tone. You will *like* everyone there, and *everyone* there will like you too. Every person you meet will feel like your new best friend forever. You will finally be valued, understood, safe. No one will kick you out or even mistreat you—not in the presence of the King! And you will never again, even once, even a little, disappoint anyone else or hurt their feelings. You will be *magnificent*, like everyone around you, for Jesus will be putting his glory upon us all. We will "obtain the glory of our Lord Jesus Christ" (2 Thess. 2:14).

Even in this life, we have already come to "the heavenly Jerusalem, and to innumerable angels in festal gathering, and to the assembly of the firstborn who are enrolled in heaven" (Heb. 12:22–23). All the followers of Jesus are there, right now, in the invisible realm. It's only an inch away. And the instant after your last breath in this dark world, you will awaken to that bright world above. You will be welcomed in. Martin Luther might laugh as he shakes your hand vigorously. Elisabeth Elliot might smile as she offers you a cup of tea. You will discover how good it feels to *deeply* belong, and your joy will never end.

Why should we, citizens of that eternal city above, fear earthly death here below? By faith in God's promises in the gospel, let's get ready now so that we face it then with calm confidence.

Let's Get Ready—Now

The Bible says, "It is appointed for man to die once, and after that comes judgment" (Heb. 9:27). Are you ready? You can be. Here's how.

Stake your eternity not on your obedience or your attainments or your virtues, but stake all your hope on the atoning work of Jesus alone. He lived for you the virtuous life you've failed to live, and he died for you the atoning death you aren't even able to die. God is offering you, freely and forever, Jesus as your better "you." When you show up at heaven's door and the angel on duty asks you why you should be allowed in, you can say, "I can't give you any good reason why someone like me should be allowed in there. But if you'll let Jesus know I'm here, *he said he'd get me in.*"

If you'll take Jesus as your only hope for the day of judgment, you *will* be judged on that day—judged as *righteous,* qualified, clothed with Jesus himself. How about it, then? Will you put all your hope in Jesus alone? He will not let you down. He is enough—forever.

Then, with heaven standing wide open to you, why not look forward to your dying day? Your death will be "but a passage out of a prison into a palace."[17] When God gives you the command, "Die," you can say, "Yes, Lord! At last!" And he will help you obey him even then—especially then.

17 John Bunyan, quoted in Leroy Garrett, "The Abolition of Death," *Restoration Review* 31, no. 3 (1989): 45, https://digitalcommons.acu.edu/.

John Wesley, the founder of the Methodist movement, said, "Our people die well. The world may find fault with our opinions, but the world cannot deny that our people die well."[18] How could it be otherwise? Jesus is preparing a place for us, and we can't wait to get there!

Peter Kreeft helps us grab on to the boldness of our hope. Here is the confidence we now have in Christ:

Now suppose both death and hell were utterly defeated. Suppose the fight was fixed. Suppose God took you on a crystal ball trip into your future and you saw with indubitable certainty that despite everything—your sin, your smallness, your stupidity—you could have free for the asking your whole crazy heart's deepest desire: heaven, eternal joy. Would you not return fearless and singing? What can earth do to you if you are guaranteed Heaven? To fear the worst earthly loss would be like a millionaire fearing the loss of a penny—less, a scratch on a penny.[19]

During World War II, a newspaper reporter asked C. S. Lewis what he would do if the German air force dropped

18 Quoted in J. C. Ryle, *The Christian Leaders of the Last Century* (London: Nelson, 1869), 173.
19 Peter Kreeft, *Heaven: The Heart's Deepest Longing* (San Francisco: Ignatius, 1980), 183.

an atomic bomb on England and Lewis saw it falling right toward him. "If you had only one last thought, what would it be?" the reporter asked. Lewis replied that he would look up at that bomb, stick his tongue out at it, and say, "Pooh! You're only a bomb. I am an immortal soul."[20]

You have every right, in Christ, to that audacious freedom of heart. It is the glory of God resting upon you, and on me, as we face death. And soon it will be your turn, and my turn. We will follow our many friends in Christ through the valley of the shadow of death, all the way into the Father's house. Jesus himself will go with us every step of the way. He knows that valley well. He walked it too.

There is no rock bottom too deep for Jesus.

And that's good news, isn't it?

Questions for Reflection and Discussion

1. As we complete our discoveries in Isaiah 57:15, what are your own favorite takeaways from this verse? And what insights do you think will help you the most for the rest of your life?

20 Peter Kreeft, *Christianity for Modern Pagans* (San Francisco: Ignatius, 1993), 56.

2. Draw up a list of contrasts between our culture's ideas about aging and death and the Bible's ideas about aging and death. And what do you see as the *practical* differences these two views tend to make?

3. What new thoughts about death and about Jesus open up to you from his experience at the tomb of Lazarus in John's Gospel, chapter 11?

4. How does the Bible change your thoughts about your own death in this world? What fears does the Bible put to rest in your heart? What hopes does the Bible inspire in your heart?

5. How do the thrilling promises of the gospel give us *courage* as we live and die in this troubled world right now? What practical and even beautiful differences does that gospel make for suffering, dying people like us?

6. As you face the unknowns of your own future, are you settled in Christ? Or are you gambling on your own wits and luck? Is there anything that holds you back from staking everything on the grace of Christ for sinful sufferers like all of us? Why not decisively trust him *now*?

7. With what prayer would you like to finalize your experience of *Good News at Rock Bottom*? What do you want to say to God *now*? Don't let this moment pass by without sealing it with a prayer to the high and holy one, who is so near to you right this moment.

Conclusion

Personal Commitment

With a Benediction

Dear Lord and Savior Jesus Christ,
I hold up all my weakness to your strength,
my failure to your faithfulness,
my sinfulness to your perfection,
my loneliness to your compassion,
my little pains to your great agony on the Cross.
I pray that you will cleanse me, strengthen me,
    guide me,
so that in all ways my life may be lived as you would
    have it lived,
without cowardice and for you alone.

Show me how to live in true humility, true contrition, and true love. Amen.[1]

_____

(signed)

_____

(date)

And the blessing of God Almighty—Father, Son, and Holy Spirit—be and abide with you, both now and forevermore. Amen.

---

1 *The Book of Common Prayer* (Huntington Beach, CA: Anglican Liturgy Press, 2019), 674.

Acknowledgments

I OWE A PROFOUND DEBT of gratitude to my dear wife, Jani, for her faithful prayers and endless encouragement. "The heart of her husband trusts in her" (Prov. 31:11). That's what the Bible says of "the valiant wife."[1] That's you, darling. Thank you.

The Board of Renewal Ministries—David and Ashley Edwards, Byron and Anne Morris, John and Melinda Perry, Howard and Dawn Varnedoe—provides wise oversight. "There is safety in having many advisers" (Prov. 11:14 NLT). I feel safe with you, friends. Thank you.

Gena Mayse, our assistant at Renewal Ministries, works diligently, cheerfully and wisely behind the scenes. I am continually "assisted by you for my journey" (Rom. 15:24 CSB). Thank you, Gena.

1 Bruce K. Waltke, *The Book of Proverbs: Chapters 15–31* (Grand Rapids, MI: Eerdmans, 2005), 520–21.

Sam Allberry, one of the pastors at Immanuel Church, got this book going. He invited me to offer a series of talks at the Wednesday evening ministry there. And—*voilà!*—here they are. "There is a friend who sticks closer than a brother" (Prov. 18:24). That's you, Sam. Thank you.

Andrew Wolgemuth, my agent, exemplifies faithful, cheerful, diligent "partnership in the gospel" (Phil. 1:5), with high standards in every respect. Thanks, Andrew.

Lawrence Kimbrough, a wise friend, rescued me from some real bloopers, especially in chapter 4. "The sweetness of a friend comes from his earnest counsel" (Prov. 27:9). Thanks, Lawrence.

The team at Crossway has been a delight to work with. In this world of bad news, here is a publisher

who brings good news,
who publishes peace. (Isa. 52:7)

Thank you, friends.

Thom Notaro, a brilliant editor on the Crossway team, went over my manuscript with a fine-tooth comb. He is "a man skillful in his work" (Prov. 22:29). Thanks, Thom.

Last but not least, this book is dedicated to the people of Immanuel Church, Nashville, and to the people of

St. Patrick's Anglican Church, Murfreesboro—the most loving churches I have ever experienced. I am so often "refreshed in your company" (Rom. 15:32). Thank you, dear friends.

General Index

Scripture Index

Also Available from Ray Ortlund

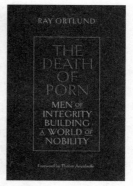

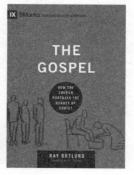

For more information, visit **crossway.org**.